BRING YOUR HAMMER

28 Tools Dads Can Grab from the Book of Nehemiah

KENT EVANS & ERIC BALLARD

Published by MJ PRESS

BRING YOUR HAMMER

Trade Paperback ISBN 978-1-949856-29-3

e-Book ISBN 978-1-949856-30-9

Published globally by Manhood Journey Press, an imprint of Manhood Journey, Inc., 212 Prestwick Place, Louisville, Kentucky 40243.

Manhood Journey and the Father & Son Circle Logo are both registered trademarks of Manhood Journey, Inc.

Printed in the United States of America.

SPECIAL SALES
Copies of *Bring Your Hammer* can be purchased at special quantity discounts when purchased in bulk by corporations, educational institutions, churches and other special-interest groups. Contact the publisher for information at info@manhoodjourney.org.

BRING YOUR HAMMER

28 Tools Dads Can Grab from the Book of Nehemiah

Endorsements

"For fatherhood to be done well, it must become who we are and why we are. In their book, *Bring Your Hammer*, Kent Evans and Eric Ballard teach the reader the life of the Old Testament leader Nehemiah, to teach us how to father our children and lead our families as God the Father intends. Using entertaining stories and a keen reflective retelling of Nehemiah's story, Evans and Ballard give today's father the path and process on how to be the father God has called us to be. *Bring Your Hammer* helps us to answer God's gift of fatherhood and to be the father he knew we would be."

Jeffrey Mason
Author of Dad, I Want to Hear Your Story:
A Father's Guided Journal to Share His Life and Love

"Eric has long been a voice I enjoy and trust. But in *Bring Your Hammer*, he and Kent have written a book that is both unique in its content and practical in its application. *Bring Your Hammer* is funny, wise, relevant, and most of all, solidly biblical. It's a book I will recommend to fathers and prospective fathers without hesitation."

Andy Blanks
Co-Founder, YM360 and Iron Hill Press

"Kent and Eric hit a core fatherhood issue head-on in *Bring Your Hammer*. Dads must learn vital fatherhood principles from Scripture, and the book of Nehemiah is full of them. Their book will help dads wield the tools they need to lead their families intentionally. Kent and Eric write in a fun style that is both engaging and challenging. If you're a dad and want to arm yourself well, grab this book!"

Tom Harper
CEO of Networld Media Group,
and author of *Servant Leader Strong:*
Uniting Biblical Wisdom and
High-Performance Leadership

"Kent and Eric have partnered together for such a time as this. Now, more than ever, men are looking for practical ways to connect to guide their sons and daughters into adulthood. Their experiences and wisdom are shared in such a way that every dad can get a real win with practical advice and transferable concepts. As dads we often need help in navigating the crazy world we live in and help our families avoid the traps and snares by rooting in them time tested values that they can apply to their everyday life. These guys have nailed it!"

Jim Whitmore
President, National Coalition of Ministries to Men

"I've been ministering to men and fathers for a long time. I know that dads need books that are practical, honest and easy to read. Men don't want lofty notions, they want actionable intelligence. In *Bring Your Hammer*, Kent and Eric provide a resource that will enable busy fathers to gain knowledge and immediately put it to use. And, this book is about one of my favorite Old Testament heroes. Nehemiah was a strong, capable and shrewd leader. Studying his life can give a dad insight and rich biblical wisdom. *Bring Your Hammer* is a great read for any dad who wants to be a godly leader of his family. Read this book!"

Clair Hoover
Executive Director,
National Coalition of Ministries to Men

"In *Bring Your Hammer*, Kent and Eric explore biblical principles dads can harvest from the book of Nehemiah. This book has no fluff - it's clear and simple. The ideas they share will help dads grow and be more intentional. Along the way, they are transparent and honest about their own lives, making the book fun to read and real. *Bring Your Hammer* has loads of practical application that a busy dad can implement right away. I highly recommend this book for dads!"

Mitch Temple, LMFT
Executive Director of the Fatherhood CoMission

Contents

Introduction

ALL FATHERS WANT TO be great.

No man embarks on the fatherhood journey just hoping he makes it as far as Average Dad Valley. No way! Lord willing, he plans to breathe his final breath atop the summit of Godly Dad Mountain.

I don't want to be a so-so leader of my family. I aspire to be a strong, influential dad who leads my family in a way that honors God. You probably feel the same way.

However, our best intentions are often dashed on the rocks of distraction, stress and conflict. Waves of struggle and self-doubt pound us as we sail through life's waters. They can drive us to a place we never intended to go, but we want more. We want to *be* more.

Inevitably, in this pursuit, we look for guidance. Hopefully, we start from a foundation that is rooted in a love for Christ, with the empowering strength of the Holy Spirit inside us. For the life of me, I can't understand how a dad navigates Fatherhood without the internal compass that is God's indwelt Spirit. He is my guide and guard.

Upon this foundation, we stack other bricks:

- The Bible
- A godly wife
- Sound teaching at our church
- Input from other dads we personally know
- Wisdom gleaned from podcasts, books, and seminars

Along the way, we sometimes find "lighthouse men." These are men anchored into the solid rock of Christ. They are stable. The beam they shine keeps us free from danger and helps us find our way. If we're wise, we spot these men and learn all we can from their example.

One of these great men is the Old Testament leader, Nehemiah.

Nehemiah was many things: governor, lawyer, pastor, worship leader, architect, and sheriff.

The one thing he wasn't, as far as we know: a Father. There's no record of Nehemiah having a family of his own.

So, why on earth write a book about an amazing Father figure *who was never actually a Father*? Because, despite not having a family of his own, Nehemiah shows us how to be a great father by modeling the character of God the Father.

Nehemiah's fatherhood example springs from his character's resemblance to God, not just from the tips and techniques he learned on the job. He shows us a great Father's heart and habits by mirroring God's heart and habits.

Ironically, I'd go a step further: Besides Jesus Himself, Nehemiah presents us with one of the most comprehensive snapshots of a godly dad in all of scripture. It's all there, in one Old Testament figure. His memoirs capture the essence of this famous fighter-lover combo, who knocked out the enemies of his day while fiercely loving those under his charge.

And, isn't that the point? If you're a dad, aren't you really a picture, an example, a shadow that represents God the Father? Aren't we dads supposed to be showing the world our godly Dad by the way we serve and love our families?

We spend too much time studying techniques of earthly dads and not enough time studying the character of God the Father. This is what we'll look at through the life of Nehemiah.

This is why we think Nehemiah's example is so useful to Fathers. Nehemiah demonstrated so many facets of the character of Almighty God. Just as there are many Hebrew words that demonstrate God's nature, from God-Provider to God-Redeemer to God-Protector; there are dozens of ways Nehemiah demonstrated God-like character.

We are going to walk through this together. Whether we're looking at Nehemiah's faith in God, his love for his people, his ability to make tough decisions, or his uncanny capacity to focus on the task at hand, we will learn lessons we can take with us on our Fatherhood journey.

We've decided to cover these traits chronologically. We'll address them in the order in which they appear within the book of Nehemiah.

There are two main reasons for this:

- Clarity: This approach kept us from creating artificial groupings that scripture doesn't give us. That wouldn't be a terrible idea, but it's a safeguard, nonetheless.
- Study: It will help you work through Nehemiah as you read this book. If you have to make a choice, commit Nehemiah to memory and forget what we write.

Oh, and who's this "we" I keep talking about? My name is Kent Evans. I'm joined on this fatherhood exposé of Nehemiah by my good friend and gifted storyteller, Eric Ballard. We tag-teamed the writing of this book. We'll try to keep you oriented along the way, so you know who's sharing in which chapters. For the most part, we each tackle whole chapters.

Together, Eric and I hope that we've done you a good service through this book. We hope it helps you appreciate the story in Nehemiah even more, but, more centrally, apply what you're reading to your own life. Like you, we want to be godly dads who lead our families in a way that honors God.

So, with that, let's dive in.

1

BY KENT

The Godly Dad **LOVES** Those Under His Care

> "...I questioned them about the Jewish remnant that had survived the exile, and also about Jerusalem."
>
> *NEHEMIAH 1:2*

NEHEMIAH WAS THE CUPBEARER to the King. The importance of this role is easy to misunderstand. Nehemiah was not just a random butler or galley servant. On the contrary, a cupbearer was a King's trusted ally. He made sure the food and drink served to the King was to his liking, but more importantly, poison free. To do this, cupbearers learned a sophisticated three-step process at the elite Ivy League Cupbearer Colleges of their day:

> *Step 1: taste food*
> *Step 2: wait a few minutes*
> *Step 3: check for your pulse*
> @susacupbearer: I'm alive! Food's good.
> #oneofthesedays

As a result of the daily risks they took, these men were well regarded. Men of integrity and honor. Their loyalty couldn't be bought, or compromised, and their devotion was unquestioned. Kings trusted cupbearers with their very lives, and by extension, the kingdom itself.

Nehemiah's focus

Nehemiah had risen to this role under King Artaxerxes of Persia. The book of Nehemiah picks up around 444 B.C., as Nehemiah's brother pays a visit to the royal palace.

We don't read of any pleasantries or hear them catching up on small talk. Nehemiah dives right in, asking how his people (the Jews) are faring. Specifically, he wondered about the city of Jerusalem. Within two verses, we already see a glimpse into Nehemiah's heart. One that's quite different from mine.

I would've opened with, "Hey bro! Check it ooouut! Is this gig off the hook, or what?! I get to serve *the King*! I've even got a company car (clean horse), the latest tech (fresh scrolls), and a fully funded 401k (burial tomb)!"

I'd have been all too happy to bask in the glow of my high position. I had "made it." Maybe Nehemiah did the same thing, and we pick up the story right after he'd given his brother the nickel tour of the primo wash basins. I doubt it. Based on the rest of the book, I don't think that's how Nehemiah rolled. He wasn't in it for himself.

His burning question: *How are my people and my city doing?*

The city of cities

Cities had unique significance in ancient times. Just like the cupbearer's role needs to be grasped to fully appreciate Nehemiah's position, the importance of a city – and the wall that surrounded it – is also crucial to understanding the rest of this story.

Sure, big cities mean something to a nation today. What would France be without Paris? England without London? Or the good ol' US of A without some of our amazing cities.

But at this point in history, cities weren't just status symbols. They were a means of protection for the citizens. Daily threats were real, and a city gave inhabitants a stronghold to keep them safe.

Watchmen stood atop the city wall to look for danger (2 Samuel 18:24-26; Ezekiel 33:1-6). The bigger the wall, the farther he could see. No city wall? No safety. But, the importance of the city wall for the Israelites ran even deeper.

A well-run city, encircled by a sturdy wall, signified the Lord's blessing on that place. If your city (or its wall) was run down, you weren't enjoying God's favor. When God's wrath was unleashed on His people, he left their wall destroyed (2 Chronicles 36:15-21).

This sent a signal to everyone: God is not pleased with these people. Just look at this place, would you?

Protection. Safety. Spiritual favor. Yet, still there's more.

Jerusalem wasn't just any city. It was *the* city. It was a symbol of Zion, where God would one day rule again in His restored earthly kingdom. Even today, Jerusalem continues to be the most hotly contested real estate on earth. God's shining city on a hill had indeed lost its luster.

If cities are stars, Jerusalem is the sun. In the grand scheme of God's creation, no city on earth holds the same significance. It's the most important city ever created.

Now, don't be offended. I've lived my whole life in Louisville, Kentucky. I love my city and the people and places found here. My wife and I are in the process of raising five "future men" (not boys!) here, and I love the roots it's given me. But, Nehemiah's love for Jerusalem runs much deeper.

He would have died for that city.

Becoming others-centric

One of our big tests as fathers is how we love those under our care. Obviously, we love our families (don't we?). But, what does that love look like? Do we put their needs above our own? Are we so concerned with their welfare that we dive into their situations and try to understand how things are

8 | KENT EVANS

going? Do we care enough that we're willing – even happy – to listen when they interrupt us?

Let's put this in a modern context. I don't ever go months without seeing my family. Certainly not years. I see them every night. Even when I'm traveling, I call or FaceTime to catch up. So, it's hard for me to imagine needing an update like, "Is our city still standing?"

But, Nehemiah cared, and he wanted an update. How can we translate that to our own roles as Dads? We probably don't need to ask our children if their school's still upright or if their church building has been leveled. So, here's what his inquiry might look like for us.

If you have young children still at home:

- You ask about friends, and check-in periodically to see how they're doing.
- You dive into technology choices, keep track of time spent and websites clicked.
- You learn about school dynamics: favorite teachers, hard subjects, upcoming tests.

If you're an empty nester:

- "Your job going okay?"
- "How are my grandkids doing?"
- "Had your cholesterol checked lately?"

Let's camp here for just a moment. Please note two things:

1. <u>He asked</u> – Nehemiah sought to understand where his "family" found themselves. He cared enough to ask. I've often been so wrapped up in my struggles, I've ignored those of my wife and five sons.

2. <u>What he asked about</u> – He asked about their welfare. He leaned in and wanted to know precisely how they were doing.

One lesson we can take from this: Dads, we need to ask our kids great questions and a ton of them!

Ask them about their thoughts, likes, friends, fears, temptations, hopes, sins, regrets. Ask them about their favorite things. Their least favorite. Ask them how you can be a better dad. Ask them what they want in their future spouse. Ask them why they need that rock-and-roll music turned up so loud.

Ask. Ask. Ask.

When they're done answering, get some sleep. Then, wake up the next day with the ask-o-cannon reloaded. One way we can demonstrate our love is by *being genuinely inquisitive*. Ask because we truly want the answers.

Proverbs 20:5 says, "The purposes of a person's heart are deep waters, but one who has insight draws them out." One who *has insight*.

Let that rattle around for a moment. Do you have insight? Do you draw out the purposes of a person's heart? Your wife? Your children?

Consider Solomon's word picture. There's a deep pool and the man with insight lowers his bucket to the bottom. He pulls up water from below. Not something you can do flippantly, or in a herky-jerky fashion. You'd spill the water. You do it slowly and intently. It takes effort.

That's how we should be engaging our families. With a love so patient that we regularly reach into their hearts and draw out their plans, purposes, and desires. This is how we know the condition of our "family wall." We ask great questions and then listen to discover where our wall is weak. What needs shoring up?

Getting outside ourselves

The goal: to think beyond and outside ourselves. Reflect back on Nehemiah's position. He had all the trappings of "corporate success." He could've become self-focused.

His job required constant vigilance. If he ever made the wrong call, and the King died, Nehemiah's head would be the next to roll. Nobody took out a King and then offered his senior advisors a contract extension. They cleaned house.

With a job this crucial, Nehemiah was certainly tempted to be completely wrapped up in it. It could've been the center of his universe. But, based on his question – and the amazing, courageous actions he takes based on the answer – we see a man who's focused on the wellbeing of everyone *but* himself.

CONSIDER THESE QUESTIONS

- Interruptions: How do you respond when you're interrupted by a family member? What does that say about your level of compassion and love toward them?

- Questions: Do you do more talking or asking? Are you diving into your family members' hearts and lives to see where their "wall" is eroding?

- Availability: Have you been so caught up in your job success that you're never around for your family? What adjustments can you make to be more available?

2

BY KENT

The Godly Dad **PRAYS** for Guidance and Wisdom

"When I heard these things, I sat down and wept. For some days I mourned and fasted and prayed before the God of heaven."

NEHEMIAH 1:4

HOW MANY PROBLEMS HAVE you encountered as a dad? Let's say you've been a dad for 10 years. Have you had as least one "issue" per day? There are those rare problem-free days, but others make up for those. Amen?

Some problems are simple: "Dad, can you open the peanut butter jar for me?"

Some are challenging: "Dad, I saw my friend cheating on a test today. What do I do now?"

Some are downright scary: "Daddy, I'm pregnant."

Allow me a baseball metaphor: some of your Dad troubles are like slow-rolling ground balls. Easily handled. Some, however, are like blazing line-drives with topspin, and just slowing them down is a mixture of skill and luck. You've probably seen a mix. And, it's likely that you've fielded thousands since bringing that first little one home.

It's also likely that the bigger the problem, the less you know about exactly how to solve it.

Praying early and often

Considering this, a question: Of the many problems you've had to solve, which ones did you pray about before you jumped into solving?

If you're like me, you just reactively dive into about 90% of them. You see prayer as a last resort. "All we can do now is pray." But Nehemiah viewed it as a first response. "When I heard this... I prayed."

And, in this chapter, let's just focus on Nehemiah's prayer. We could also look at fasting and mourning (weeping) as well. But we don't have time for everything and talking about fasting makes me hungry.

Some of our prayer omissions might be understandable. I mean, do you really need, "Dear God, please give me skill to remove this jar lid, in Jesus' name." Of course, your every breath is under God's control, so you could meet your end while fumbling with the jar. In which case, your child would be scarred for life, having watched you keel over just because they asked you to help them make a sandwich. They'd hate peanut butter forever! A real tragedy.

Wow. Sorry. I got a bit off-track. Welcome to the inner workings of my mind. But, just to close the point: peanut butter is awesome. Unless you have a nut allergy. If that's you, sorry you're denied the blessing here on earth. I'm sure God will give you a peanut butter buffet in heaven as payback. (pro tip: go for crunchy).

Getting back to the point – of the zillion problems that have ended up on your Fatherhood plate (get it!?), how many did you prayerfully address? What percentage do you normally submit to God?

Nehemiah heard about the distress of his people. Immediately, he weeps, mourns, fasts and prays. He says, "for *some days* I mourned, fasted and prayed...". He didn't just toss up a desperate, "God help us!" He humbled himself and sought God's favor.

We see a recap of his prayer in Nehemiah 1:5-11. In it, he projects humility, confesses his sins (more on that later), reminds God of his promises, and finally asks God for favor with the King.

Nehemiah realized the problem he faced was too big for him to fix by himself.

Not only that. He didn't just need God's help to move a mountain. More fundamentally, he acknowledged he was a sinner who needed God's forgiveness.

It went like, "Dear God, You are awesome, please listen to me, I'm a mess, and so are my people…" A radically humble approach. He interceded for them, but, in the process, admitted his inadequacy to play that role.

If we were outlining Nehemiah's prayer approach, it might look like this:

- God, You're awesome
- Please listen
- I know I'm a sinner
- But <u>you said</u>, when we repent, you'll help
- I'm asking you to help us
- Specifically, here's how

In the timeless hit song on sin, humility and forgiveness (obviously: "Gimme Three Steps"), Lynyrd Skynyrd begs his opponent, "And I know you don't owe me, but I wish you'd let me ask one favor from you…" The wayward dancer's only hope was an appeal to the good character of the man in charge (aka, the guy with the gun). Just give me a head start.

Besides Nehemiah's appropriate humility, don't miss this: Nehemiah knew God's ways.

Calling on God's promises

Woven into this prayer is a glimpse of how deeply Nehemiah understood God's nature and His love for his people. Nehemiah's dropping a small reminder, "Hey, God – it was your idea to redeem and forgive. Remember that? You said if we turned to you, you'd help. Well, I'm turning to you. Me and some other folks. So, could you come through for us, as in, right now?"

There's often no better prayer than one which uses God's own words. And, this isn't some reading back of the court reporter's notes. We don't play "Gotcha!" with God. His promises aren't some trap door He's standing over while we hold the lever. He's under no obligation as to when & how He redeems or restores.

He may allow everyone to die, but, redeem them at the last second like the thief on the cross. He may not save His people, but instead use their death to turn the hearts of their attackers toward him as He did the Apostle Paul's. That's His call.

Even so, we see Nehemiah calling on that character in his time of need. He knew God's promises. By knowing them, it enabled him to pray in a directed, powerful fashion that put God's righteousness and character on full display.

The prayer that packs a punch is one focused on God's character, His words, His name. Not primarily on our benefit. Rather, on the magnification of God's glory. "God, please intervene, for the sake *of your promises* to your people, not because they *deserve* it."

How can we call on God's promises if we don't know them?

Closing with a specific ask

Nehemiah's first chapter concludes with this prayer, "'Give your servant success today by granting him favor in the presence of this man.' I was cupbearer to the king."

Nehemiah doesn't just end with "your will be done," even though that's sometimes appropriate. He wants something specific and timely. Something only God can do: grant him favor with the king. In our modern era – and in a democratic society – we need to pause in order to realize how important "favor with the king" would be to someone like Nehemiah.

On one hand, as the cupbearer, he does have the King's ear. He has "general favor." By virtue of his continued employment, he was in the King's good graces. But, here, Nehemiah is asking for something much more tangible.

The next interaction Nehemiah will have with the king occurs about four months after his brother's visit. I'm grateful God chose to preserve this tiny time-lapse detail. We'll look more deeply at some things that transpired during those four months in later chapters. For now, suffice it to say that Nehemiah's prayer indicates he was ready to "pitch" the King an idea and he was asking God to go before him.

"Today's the day, God. Please give him open ears."

Have you ever needed favor with a person who held the keys to something really important for you?

We've adopted two boys from Ethiopia. As part of that process, we were entirely dependent on favor with many people and organizations. Adoption overseers in country, social workers, and embassies all hold powerful sway over how quickly (or whether) your case moves through. It can be a grueling process of waiting and wondering.

This all comes to a head in your "court date." That's when you're finally heading to the main courthouse in Addis Ababa, Ethiopia's capital. You queue up and wait for your name to be called. Then, you enter humbly according to the instructions from your adoption liaison. Don't say much, no kidding around, answer the questions. Keep it quick.

This person will determine whether this little orphan becomes your child. Once he or she signs off, the legal tables tilt in your favor. It's basically a formality from there on out.

God, grant me favor today with this judge.

We did this twice. Each time I was mindful of what was at stake. It's a powerful moment of abject humility. If this judge decided to halt our case, we'd have very few options. Most wouldn't end well. We needed his signature.

I love how Bible commentator Matthew Henry says it, "Those that would find favour with kings must secure the favour of the King of kings."

Nehemiah was about to enter the King's presence. He had a plan. He would share his plan if the King would listen. And his request was going to be huge.

He needed favor with this man, so he prayed.

CONSIDER THESE QUESTIONS

- How's your prayer life going? Do you find yourself regularly talking to and with God? What one thing could you do this week to be more prayer-centric?

- When you consider Nehemiah's example, are you praying for stuff with an attitude of entitlement, or are you humbly asking God to help? How could you improve here?

- Recall a time when you prayed for something that didn't end up the way you wanted. Did this cause you to question God? Talk to Him about that now.

3

The Godly Dad **CONFESSES** his Own Sin First

> "...I confess the sins we Israelites, including myself and my father's family, have committed against you."
>
> *NEHEMIAH 1:6*

WE COULD LOOK AT a number of aspects of Nehemiah's prayer. A few, we addressed in the previous chapter. Allow me to select one I think will help and perhaps surprise us. Nehemiah confesses his own sin first.

I used to work for an advertising agency. We often pulled long hours. Occasionally, we'd take a short break, especially in the evenings. One night, we were playing paddleball in the lobby. I was goofing off and tossed my paddle toward the ball. Shockingly, it took flight. It kept going and going until it rocketed into the all-glass front door.

In one sense, it was amazing. Tempered glass really does shatter into a zillion tiny pieces. Good safety feature. Yet, I was mortified. Not only would I probably have to cover the costs to fix the door, I'd be digging that money out of my final paycheck once they fired me.

I knew the only way to handle this was with a preemptive strike. I cleaned up the mess. Then, I went into the agency president's office (a hard-driving, aggressive businesswoman) and left her a note. I apologized, took responsibility, and offered to pay for the door.

The next morning, I came in early and waited for my phone to ring. Sure enough, when she arrived, I saw her buzz in. I answered. She was laughing. Huh? She blurted, "Hey Kent! I got your note. That's *#@!! hilarious. Don't worry about the door, we'll get it fixed. So #!!!@# funny." She hung up. That was it. No lengthy diatribe about my irresponsibility or how much front doors cost these days. We were done.

Months later, when April and I were married, that same (teddy bear on the inside) lady gave me "unlimited" frequent flier miles as my wedding gift. Free trip to Hawaii! One simple confession scored me some points and made me an even more valuable employee to the big boss.

I didn't apologize in order to gain points. And, Nehemiah wasn't trying to score any either. He just acknowledged his sinfulness before Almighty God. He doesn't sugar coat it either. He got right to the point.

If we're going to be the leaders God wants us to be, we need to get our sin out in the open before God. It's a prerequisite for godly leadership.

Humility is the cornerstone from which God builds great leaders. Not only do we need *to know* our sin, we need *to say* it to God. And if we neglect to do this, we constrict our relationship with Him. Not only that, we risk putting a barrier up between God and our children. Let me explain.

Get flattened

I love the main New Testament word for humble: *tapeinoō*. Partly, it's just fun to look at. Even funner to say: teh-pie-NAH-oh!

Jesus said, "The greatest among you will be your servant. For those who exalt themselves will be *humbled (tapeinoō)*, and those who *humble (tapeinoō)* themselves will be exalted." (Matthew 23:11-12).

Exalt yourself, get humbled. And, vice versa. Got it.

Then, look at its usage in Luke 3:5, "Every valley shall be filled in, every mountain and hill *made low (tapeinoō)*. The crooked roads shall become straight, the rough ways smooth." This is a reference to John the Baptist. He would prepare the way for the Messiah. The hills will be "made low." They'll be "humbled."

As Christ was coming to earth, in God's divine plan, the "ground" was made level to facilitate the Messiah's arrival.

Clearly, this is a spiritual reality. John the Baptist wasn't operating a backhoe down by the Jordan River. Instead, he was part of God's plan to smash down the hardened hearts of those awaiting the arrival of the Christ.

A blunt way to look at how I'm made humble: I will be pounded flat. My heart is the bumpy terrain. God's spirit is the asphalt paver. He's going to roll over me, back and forth, continuing to make me humble. Sometimes in the same spot! To "flatten" me.

Does He do this just because He enjoys it? Is God like an asphalt paving rodeo cowboy who just loves squashing us under his mighty wheel? Yee-haw!

No. He humbles us because level ground is *the best surface to build on.*

Ready for building

No contractor worth his salt builds on uneven, unstable terrain. Even those who build houses on mountainsides must set footers and pillars in something solid to give them a stable base as a starting point.

The work being done in your heart is similar. The biggest difference between our hearts and real construction is this: In actual construction, the builder gets the surface level and then builds on it. Straightforward. For our hearts, though, it's an ongoing process. Humble us. Build some. Humble us again (same spot, really?). Build some more. On and on.

God's sanctifying work in our hearts *continually humbles us.* Our hearts are being increasingly prepared for more building. He keeps smoothing out our hearts and minds with each pass of his loving (and often painful) steamroller.

Why is this so important to understand as a dad? Because our own "uneven surface" may accidentally become the biggest roadblock to the spiritual growth of our children. We will be the pile of rocks impeding their pursuit of a rich and rewarding faith.

The reason: humility and hypocrisy are connected.

Hypocrisy's antidote

Many talented researchers have documented reasons that cause our children to choose (or abandon) the faith they were exposed to in our homes. There's not just one factor. Our enemy finds increasingly diabolical approaches:

- Confusing messages sent by culture and social media
- Legalistic preachers who give our kids no room to grow or be restored
- Insidious exposure to damaging content
- Overly permissive parents who downplay the value of righteous living

But, of all the forces at work to derail our children, there's one we Fathers should focus on the most: *our own walk with the LORD.*

Many of these researchers have pointed to hypocrisy as a key reason our kids abandon their faith. In some cases, they're citing hypocrisy within the church. But, often it's *hypocrisy in our own homes* causing our kids to question whether the Christian life is for real.

They wonder, "If my parents go to church, smile and shake hands; but then, on the ride home, they rail against the preacher, elders or the color of the carpet, what's that about? Do I really want a part in 'that kind' of Christian life?"

> *Hey Dad: your personal authenticity can significantly influence the spiritual trajectory of your children. If you're regularly immersed in God's Word, your kids will sense it. If you're frequently praying for them, they'll know it. If you're loving your wife as Christ loved the church, they'll want a marriage like that.*

This is why humility and hypocrisy are inextricably linked. If we're humble, we'll be able to be "real" with our families. When we've done something well, we can praise God and share the joy. When we've blown it, we can ask for forgiveness and move on. We can be real.

Our kids will sense that our faith is not lip service, and that kind of faith is attractive. Clearly, there's no guarantee. You can't be a perfect dad who cranks out perfect kids. What a laugh. But, authenticity clears the bridge. They still must walk across.

We insist, "Share with your brother," as we fling the offering plate past us. We encourage, "Be nice to your teachers," but every night at dinner we criticize our boss. We rebuke, "Stop gossiping," then moments later when we think they're out of earshot, we start in with our wife, "Did you hear why Bill and Mary are splitting up?"

We must fully accept this reality: our kids rarely embrace a faith "more real" than our own. Sure, God can do anything. He is sovereign. But, why test Him? Why spray spiritual Round Up in our homes and make it harder for seeds of faith to sprout?

Hypocrisy in one generation frequently yields outright rebellion in the next.

Start with our own mess

Nehemiah didn't start with, "Dear God, I know my people are wayward and obstinate, but please have mercy *on them.*" How often have we as Fathers leaned into our kids' lives to rebuke them, while not at the same time realizing that we too are sinners?

Let's say your son is caught cheating at school. You have to address it. He needs correction and likely some serious consequences. What if you prayed before stepping into his room?

> *"Dear God, You are the God of truth and honesty. Please hear me. I want to help my son learn from this experience. But, I too am a cheater! I've cheated You with my time, money, and relationships. I'm not perfect in this area. Thank you for the mercy you've shown me. Give me wisdom right now."*

We see Nehemiah modeling personal humility in a way that should both convict and encourage us. By placing the humility cornerstone down – and repeatedly resetting it – we put our hearts on a level plain and invite God to work through us in a powerful way.

That's a foundation God loves to build on.

CONSIDER THESE QUESTIONS

- When was the last time you confessed your sin to God? Isn't it about time you do it again?

- How have you been hypocritical to your family? Can you think of at least one way? Would you be willing to bring it up with them and get it out in the open?

- What areas in your life have you found yourself resisting his humble steamroller? Where have you obstinately refused to change?

4

BY KENT

The Godly Dad **APPEALS** to God for Provision

> "Remember the instruction you gave your servant Moses..."
>
> *NEHEMIAH 1:8*

CONSIDER TWO VERY DIFFERENT prayers of a Father:

"Dear God, my son is coming up on finals this week at school. Please give him full remembrance of all that he has learned and confidence as he takes his test. This way, he will ace his class, finish out his 4.0, and solidify that college scholarship we so desperately need. Amen."

Or...

"Dear God, you've promised to never leave or forsake us! I'm so grateful. This week, please be with my son and allow him to live and work and study for your glory. You said you are our guide and our peace, so this week, please be that calm, still voice in my son's heart. Amen."

Right now you may be wondering, "Didn't we talk about prayer in Chapter 2? And, then confession in Chapter 3? Can't these guys leave this prayer topic alone? Do they think I'm not paying attention? That I can't read?!"

Your words, pal. Not ours. And stop yelling at us. You know, we're not really there with you, right? Here you are talking to a book. Who's not paying attention now?

Indeed, what we're seeing in Nehemiah 1:8 is similar to what we've seen in the prior few verses. But, previously, we talked about focusing on praying and how confession can be a key part in that. Great stuff. Now, let's take a deeper dive into how we pray and what we pray for.

Before we get too far, let me be clear. Any time we pray to God is time well spent. There are no perfect prayers. If God only listened to perfect prayers lifted up by perfect people, He'd never tune in. But, some of our conversations with Him are more selfish and pettier than we'd like to admit. Let's be honest, we can toss up some ideas that are odd at best, and occasionally selfish at worst.

Read through the Psalms to see some very interesting requests the Psalmist makes of God. Here's just one: "In your unfailing love, silence my enemies; destroy all my foes, for I am your servant." (Psalm 143:12). No punches pulled there.

God loves when we come to him with our fears, concerns, wishes, and mistakes. Open, honest, and completely vulnerable. He loves us despite our disposition and intentions. That's what grace is all about.

Even so, take another look at the two prayers of a father above. How would you compare those prayers? What's the heart behind each of them?

In the first prayer, the aim of the request is earthly reward, achievement and a favorable outcome for the father's child (and, by extension, the family budget).

What a great thing to pray for! If anything, we fathers pray way too little for our families. We need to be on our knees asking God for everything from spiritual provision to safe travel to godly spouses to positive lab results. At various points in the lives of my children, I've prayed prayers just like that one.

Yet, notice that second prayer. Let's compare it to what we see in the life of Nehemiah. Notice what Nehemiah's doing here in verse eight. He's asking God to remember the instruction He gave Moses. Isn't that interesting?

"Remember the instruction you gave your servant Moses, saying, 'If you are unfaithful, I will scatter you among the nations, but if you return to me and obey my commands, then even if your exiled people

are at the farthest horizon, I will gather them from there and bring them to the place I have chosen as a dwelling for my Name.' They are your servants and your people, whom you redeemed by your great strength and your mighty hand." (Nehemiah 1:8-10)

Did God forget?

Is Nehemiah reminding God of something that God has forgotten? When God hears Nehemiah's prayer, does God say, "Oh my goodness?! I'm so glad you mentioned that, Nehemiah! I'd gotten so busy running the universe, that I completely forgot I said it. I don't know what I'd do without your great memory! Thank you so much, you're a champ."

Um, no. God's not forgetful. About anything. Ever.

Nehemiah is setting the prayer table by recalling those instructions. It's not something God has forgotten, but it is something that Nehemiah wants to reestablish as he petitions God for something else. We will see that in a moment.

Have you ever promised your kids something that they remembered, but you forgot? Just a couple nights ago, my five-year-old son wanted to look for his Batman cape at bedtime. We have piles and piles of "costume" items in various places in our house. There was no way I was going on the cape-goose-chase at bedtime. So, I said, "You bet, Titus. You go on to sleep, and we'll look for it tomorrow."

I figured, he's only five. He'll totally forget that after a good night's sleep. I was wrong. He woke up, came and found me with this greeting, "You said, 'tomorrow we can find your cape.'" He was quoting me like a court reporter. You know precisely what I said next, don't you? "Go ask your mom where it is." He replied, "She just told me to ask you." Checkmate.

Maybe you've let your children down too. And, maybe it was not something like helping them find a costume accessory. More than likely, you've made your family hundreds of promises, big and small. And, if you're like me, you've dropped the ball on more than a few of them.

Sometimes, you blow it because you simply forget, and the consequences are small. Other times, not following through on our promises can be disastrous. We've all felt the pain of broken promises. In many cases, we need only look in the mirror to see the reason. From time to time, we need to be reminded of our promises and held accountable.

And, this is the spirit behind Nehemiah's prayer. He's not trying to use God's words against Him as much as he's calling upon God's gracious and loving character to follow through, as He's indicated he would.

How did Nehemiah know?

Nehemiah knew what God had promised to Moses. Consider this for a moment. Nehemiah lived thousands of years after Moses. How would he have known about these promises? Through at least two ways.

First, he would've heard stories passed down from his own parents and grandparents. He'd have listened as faithful ancestors shared tales of the plagues, the Red Sea and the Ten

Commandments. Second, he would've read about them in the scriptures and historical texts himself. Through careful study, he would have learned what God had promised.

Because Nehemiah listened to stories from those before him, and read God's scriptures, he could call upon God to fulfill what he had promised.

The implication here is obvious and stirring. How can we as Fathers and husbands call upon God to work in His ways, execute His will, and fulfill His promises if we don't know His ways, His will, or His promises?

Do God's promises include easy lives free from stress? Does He promise that our families will not struggle? That our kids will always get good grades? Or, that our wives will never have health challenges? No.

He doesn't promise us pain-free lives. However, He does promise He will never leave or forsake us (Deuteronomy 31:6). He promises to be with us to the end of the age (Matthew 28:20). He promised us a helper, the Holy Spirit, who will guide us into all truth (John 16:13). He promises that we will have eternal life (John 3:16).

What to pray for

I was discussing prayer recently with my oldest son. We were talking about how we often misunderstand the nature and purpose of prayer. Our evidence? The fact that other believers (and non-believers) often ask, "Does prayer really work?"

Does prayer "*work*"? What kind of question is that? By work, do we mean that prayer gets things done? As in, if I pray for health or money, I get health and money? Is that what we mean by "work"?

If we view prayer as a request-o-matic – where we ask for stuff, and then hold our hand out by the divine dispenser as we wait for the delivery – I believe we're missing the point of prayer.

Indeed, God asks us to bring requests to Him. Paul tells us to submit our requests to God (Philippians 4:6), and James reminds us that the fervent prayer of a righteous man is effective (James 5:16). We see dozens of Biblical examples where people asked God to intercede on their behalf.

Definitely, prayer *includes the concept* of making requests to God. But I'd argue that *it is not limited to* that idea. And, often those requests are ones related to spiritual growth, eternal deliverance, and earthly unity with other believers. Not just good grades, financial success and physical safety.

Fathers, we must regularly intervene in prayer on behalf of our wives and children. As we do, let's pray for His will for their lives, not just for tidy situational outcomes. Let's ask him to give them the peace that passes understanding (Philippians 4:7), the wisdom to make great choices (Proverbs 3:5-6), the patience to overlook an offense (Proverbs 19:11), the courage to face challenges (Joshua 1:9), and the assurance of their eternal destiny (Romans 8:16).

Let's discuss with God *His promises* for our family. Then, we will see Him move mightily in their lives, for the sake of His own glory!

CONSIDER THESE QUESTIONS

- How well do you know God's promises? If you had to list five or ten things right now that God promises to His children, could you do it (without Googling it!)?

- How often do you pray His promises over your children – whether you're with them, or by yourself?

- Do you see prayer as a conversation or a request machine? What can you do to bring your understanding of prayer into alignment with scripture?

5

BY KENT

The Godly Dad **ASKS** Influential People for Help

"...The king said to me, 'What is it you want?'."

NEHEMIAH 2:4

IT CAN BE HUMBLING to ask for someone's help. Especially when that someone is a powerful leader. While God is no respecter of persons, some people have more sway than others. They're not more valuable or better. They're just more influential.

We can sometimes be intimidated by these individuals. They're busy. They have unlisted numbers and private email addresses. They may even be surrounded by people whose job is to keep folks like you and me away from them! "He's on vacation again? Fourth time this month!"

But, sometimes, we need their help. Not anyone else's, just theirs. We need their specific support to remove a barrier, open a door, or get access to needed supplies. No one else can do what they can do.

I remember asking a prominent government leader to be the keynote speaker for our nonprofit fundraiser. Well, to be more accurate, I had a friend of mine ask him. Why? Because they knew each other. I figured a request from a friend would go farther than mine out of the blue.

Sure enough, the leader agreed to do the speech. I was thrilled. Eventually, he and I met to discuss the event. He offered, "Kent, what would you like me to cover during my talk? How do you want this to go?"

Whoa. Here was a guy with thousands of people and billions of dollars under his leadership, and he was asking me what *I wanted him* to cover. I was pleasantly surprised, but I wasn't caught flat-footed. I showed him a couple slides I'd prepared. We talked through how he would approach his presentation.

I'd followed Nehemiah's example. When this influential man asked me what I wanted, I had an answer. When I got my shot, I was ready to pop the question.

Side note: While I haven't flown on Air Force One or been to the secret retreats of society's rich and famous, I have been around my share of influential leaders. I've discovered one thing they almost all have in common. They love a straight-up request. Don't hem and haw. Get to the point. What do you want? Spit it out, man!

If you're heading into a meeting with someone who has the unique role or capacity to help you with your mission, be ready to make the ask. In the next chapter, we'll look at Nehemiah's specific requests. But, for now, let's mine some Fatherhood lessons out of just *the asking* part.

As we do, keep this in mind: Nehemiah was taking a risk. He was putting his credibility on the line just by asking. He could lose his job – and maybe his freedom – just for asking at all. The question itself could stoke the ire of a man like Artaxerxes.

"You forgotten your place, Nehemiah? Last time I checked, I have a kingdom to run, and your job is to keep me safe while I run it. I need a cupbearer, not a freethinker whining about his past life. We're on GO here, Bud, and that means forward. Get focused. Keep your head in the game! Wanna go back to Jerusalem? Fine. I'll send you back in a box."

Okay, Artaxerxes wasn't some deranged mob boss. However, it would've been well within his rights to put Nehemiah in his place and deny him even an audience to discuss the matter. One more reason I admire Nehemiah's character and heart.

Let's look at three practical lessons for fathers from Nehemiah's approach to the King.

Acknowledge your limitations

Nehemiah had a powerful role, to be sure. However, he couldn't command the army, grant himself time off or allocate resources to a project. Only the king could do that. By approaching the King, Nehemiah was admitting his need. His personal talents would only take him so far. He couldn't get to where he wanted to go without some intervention.

This is often true for us as Fathers in a practical sense. If we're going to provide for our families, we need a job, and sometimes we need to carry our hat in our hands and go find one. If we're going to help our kids land that scholarship, we need to approach the organization or university with a humble heart and ask the right questions. We need to shelve our pride and put ourselves at the mercy of others from time to time.

This is also true in a spiritual context. Not only do we approach earthly leaders for needed physical resources, but we also approach our heavenly Father for spiritual provision. He tells us to come boldly to the throne of grace (Hebrews 4:16) and to present our requests to him (Philippians 4:6-7). Our ability to approach the king of heaven should embolden us when we approach "kings" on earth.

It all starts with humility. Are we ready to admit we don't really "got this"?

Realize the king's influence

Nehemiah knew specifically which things the king could help with. There would be things beyond the king's control – like how the Jews in Jerusalem might welcome (or not welcome) Nehemiah when he arrived. But for many other things, the king could make them happen with just a word.

There are times when it's hard to even figure out who has the influence we need. I mentioned our two international adoptions. One was smooth as silk, the other, fraught with delay and frustration. The biggest challenge in the second case was figuring out who on earth had the ability to get things done! At times, we were caught in a tempest of buck-passing-and-unempowered-people with no authority to move things forward. It took all our prayers and diligence – and some divine intervention – to find someone with enough influence to get us straight answers. It was maddening.

In an earthly context, we might need to scratch and claw our way to figure out who can unlock certain doors. Just finding the guy with the right key can be 90% of the battle. But, in a larger context, we know the one who holds the keys even to the gates of hell. We know the owner of the cattle on a thousand hills. We know the one who has not only the power to kill, but the power to save for eternity.

We don't need an org chart to see who's on top of mankind. We already know that our Father in heaven rules all rulers and that his Son is the King of Kings. He has the power to solve any problem we're having.

Build strong relationships

I had a friend in high school who went on to play Major League Baseball. In high school, he was an unassuming and friendly young man. He didn't really change much, even after a fifteen-year professional career. He was the same humble and helpful guy he was when we were teenagers.

During the height of his baseball career, he was a popular guy. People wanted his time, attention, or maybe just his autograph. He simply couldn't give time and attention to everyone who sought after it.

One time, he agreed to meet me before a game so we could get some autographs on items we were using at a charity auction. He gave me directions to the player's parking lot. I met him there a few hours before a game. I took my dad with me. When we rolled up, there were dozens of fans outside a big fence clamoring for each arriving players' attention.

My friend pulled in behind the private gate and exited his car. He waved to the fans who were shouting his name and said, "Sorry guys! I can't hang out right now." Then, he walked over to the guard and whispered something in his ear.

The guard stood up and headed toward the security gate. He pointed to me and my dad, and said, "You guys, come with me." We passed through the throng, he opened the gate, let just the two of us in, and closed it behind us.

I must tell you – that was a blast. I know it's petty and ridiculous, but it was really fun being invited "on the inside." The few dozen fans were wondering who we were and why we were so special.

Who were we? Nobody, really. We didn't have enough talent, money, or power to be invited inside the gate.

Why were we so special? Because we had a relationship. It was who we knew, and even better, who *knew us*. Because my friend had authority to either deny or accept visitors, he allowed us to borrow his authority and be welcomed in. Our relationship to the man with the keys was what got us inside that gate.

I didn't build a relationship with this guy when he was a teenager so I could one day get some cool memorabilia signed. I built the relationship with him because I liked him and enjoyed his approach to life. He was (and still is) just a good guy. Once he had fame, money and power, he already trusted me and knew I wouldn't leverage our friendship just so I could gain something.

For us fathers, we need to be regularly building relationships with everyone we can. And, not just so that one day we can leverage the relationship and ask for something. That's not the point. The point is that by the time we might need something – or, by the time that *they might need something* from us – we'll have the relational bridge building well underway.

CONSIDER THESE QUESTIONS

- What relationships do you have that can be beneficial to your family? Would your children grow from being around those people? If so, set it up.

- When was a time you needed something from an influential person? How did it go? Were you ready? What would you do differently next time?

- Are you in a position of power that could be leveraged to benefit someone else? If so, how could you open that door and help them?

6

BY KENT

The Godly Dad **PREPARES** a Strategic Game Plan

> "...I answered the king, 'If it pleases the king and if your servant has found favor in his sight, let him send me to the city...' "
>
> *NEHEMIAH 2:5*

I ONCE WORKED FOR a rapidly growing company led by a dynamic CEO. He was extremely busy. Every now and then, he'd want to dispatch me on a project or get my input. My phone would buzz, and he'd ask, "Hey, can you pop-over for a few minutes?"

I kept a file folder in one of those desktop sorters. It was labeled, "Questions for Steve." Whenever I thought of something I wanted his input on, if it wasn't urgent, I'd write it on a running list I kept in the folder. Then, when the "pop-over-here" call came, I'd snatch the folder and start walking the fifty feet to his office.

On the walk, I'd look in the folder and quickly review my list. Given the issues of the day or the season of the business, I'd pick one or two that were most important and cram them into my short-term memory. I'd shut the folder and enter his office.

After we addressed whatever it was that he called me about – usually it took just a few minutes – he'd thank me and tell me to beat it and get back to work. Just before I left, I'd say, "Oh, while I got you, do you have time for a quick question?" He'd almost always give me the time, and I'd rattle off one or two things from the file.

This was rudimentary, but highly effective. I didn't normally need a zillion big things from him, but I occasionally did want either his perspective, influence or provision. The best time to ask him was face-to-face, and right after I'd agreed to jump on whatever he'd just assigned me. I rarely went into his office without at least one agenda item of my own.

A man with a plan

This stretch in Nehemiah is one of my favorite portions. It reveals something about Nehemiah that I think is sorely

46 | KENT EVANS

missing in our society, and especially in the lives and minds of fathers. To fully appreciate it, we need a quick primer on the Hebrew calendar.

Nehemiah 1:1 provides two specific date-based references: the month (Kislev) and the year (twentieth) when Nehemiah's brother visited the capital. Then, again, in Nehemiah 2:1, we see two more dates: a new month (Nisan), same year. The duration between Kislev and Nisan was five months. How interesting.

I'm delighted God preserved this little gem for us. Such a specific timeframe. Nehemiah had probably seen the King at least one hundred times over the course of those five months. Why did he let five months pass between learning of the problem to mentioning it to the king?

I think it's because Nehemiah was a busy-busy-bee during those in-between months. He was formulating not only a plan to rebuild the wall in Jerusalem, but he was analyzing everything he'd need to accomplish the project. He'd need physical resources, vacation days and the king's authority to pass through certain places. Nehemiah thought of it all.

And, just my hunch, but I bet he didn't do this on his own. He would have rubbed elbows with some of the kingdom's best thinkers and planners. He probably had his share of Starbucks meetings with them to discuss specifics. "If I gotta build a gate about, oh I don't know, 'yay' tall, how many of those big trees will I need to cut down?"

And, consider the genius of his requests. I mean, if you had the opportunity, would you rather ask your boss for a raise, or, ask him for *permission to decide all raises*? It's the key that opens all the other doors. Nehemiah didn't just ask for a pallet of two-by-fours, he asked for permission to give orders to the keeper of the royal forest!

As fathers, there's a word I want us to remember when we read this portion of Nehemiah: intentionality. Nehemiah didn't just bring the problem to the king, "Yeah, wall's busted and I'm ticked off about it!" He didn't just bring some half-baked idea to the king, "I say we, um, maybe rebuild the wall! Yeah, that's it!" Instead, he brought the plan to fully fix the problem, "King A, here's what I want to do, and here's precisely what I'll need to do it."

Think solutions, not problems

Let's consider a common problem we've all dealt with inside our families: selfishness. Our young kids don't share their toys, or they won't offer to help around the house. We lament, "Wow! These kids are so selfish! When will they ever learn?"

Now, let's take a Nehemiah-inspired approach to this problem.

Problem: selfish kids.

Solution: Lecture on altruism? Might help. Less selfishness? Sure. But perhaps more to the point, they need to *be more oth-ers-centered*. As opposed to saying they need less selfishness,

48 | KENT EVANS

what if we said they needed more others-centeredness? This subtle shift yields tectonic results. It unlocks our ability to create action steps.

Action steps:
- Take them through a quick devotional (or full Bible study) on their identity, sinfulness and selfish hearts, and talk about how God wants to redeem that.

- Get them around others who are unselfish – encourage your teen daughter to grab lunch with that missionary who's back in the US on furlough.

- Do a local project together – clean up a park or cut the elderly neighbor's grass. Anything that's selfless or service oriented.

- Go on a mission trip together – find a need, raise support, and get them out of their comfort zone to give their time and energy to others.

The goal is not to try and *remove selfishness*, but to *implant selflessness*. Far more actionable.

Our brains really struggle to run from a negative character trait. "I wish I weren't so rash and reckless!" They're more fully engaged when we're actively chasing a picture of who we want to become. "I really want to be more patient."

This is just one example of a common issue for fathers and how we might use a more proactive approach to solve it. I'm not suggesting every single thing in our families can be solved with intentional planning. However, I do believe that we fathers think our hands are tied more often than they really are. The barrier isn't always that we don't have any options, but whether we'll take the time and energy to think them through and ask for help if we're stuck.

This is what amazes me about Nehemiah at this early stage of the book. He heard about the problem, and shortly after repenting and asking for God's mercy, he dove into what a solution might look like. Quietly, privately, patiently. He got his ducks in a row so one day he'd be ready to pop the question.

Problem finders are a dime a dozen

How many dads do you know lamenting their circumstances? Their wives aren't interested enough in sex. Their kids never talk to them. Their bosses are demanding and unreasonable. Their preachers don't cover the right topics. Their teams don't run the right plays. I know a lot of those dads. I've lamented some of those things myself.

I was at an event once that was tailored to fathers. It was terrific. During one of the breaks, a guy commented to me, "You know, we should have a similar event for the Moms." I could tell by his tone, that was the extent of it. It was a cavalier comment, not a personal commitment. He wasn't going to follow-up, take the lead, or make any effort to actually do it. He was just making conversation.

I'm not judging the guy, but I am becoming more aware of what comes out of my mouth. Especially when it even begins to remotely sound like a complaint or critique. Do I have a plan to fix it? Am I willing to jump in and help? Will I be part of the solution?

I had a boss who used to say, "People who can tell me what's broken are a dime a dozen. But people who can put together a responsible plan to fix stuff, I pay them top dollar."

So often in our families, we become the CPS, the Chief Problem Spotter. We see and sometimes vocally declare what all the problems are. "Why can't you be more responsible? Why don't you tell me what you're thinking? When will you learn how to talk respectfully? How on earth does our money keep running out before the end of the month?"

We are problem-rich and idea-poor.

A godly, intentional dad spots problems. That's key. But then, he at least makes an earnest attempt to craft a solution. He looks for resources, ideas, people with certain skills, events, books, podcasts and YouTube videos. He dives into the Bible and spends time in prayer. He seeks wisdom, guidance and, in some cases, God's direct intervention.

Nehemiah didn't sit around and whine about the problem. He got busy. He thought hard. He crossed his t's and dotted his i's. He prayerfully planned until he could plan no more. Then, he found himself in a conversation and, just like that, his plan spun into motion.

Dear dad, learn from Nehemiah's example. If he can determine every resource he'd need to rebuild a city wall in five months, surely you and I can come up with a game plan to get our kids to stop texting their friends at the dinner table, right?

CONSIDER THESE QUESTIONS

- What's a nagging issue or problem in your family that you wish were gone? Have you given up, or can you take a new step toward trying to solve it?

- Can you think of one undesirable character trait in each of your family members. One by one. Now, what is the "opposite" of that trait? How can you encourage growth in that positive trait in each person?

- What's one goal your family has in the next five years? Maybe it's to pay off debt or take an epic vacation. Do you have written plan to get there? If not, build one now, even if it's just a rough draft.

7

BY ERIC

The Godly Dad **PROVIDES** Life-Giving Resources

"...may I have letters to the governors of Trans-Euphrates, so that they will provide me safe-conduct..."

NEHEMIAH 2:7

WHEN I BECAME ENGAGED to my wife, maybe 27 seconds after she said yes, we went into wedding planning mode. I say "we," but in reality, she did everything. The only thing I was in charge of was picking out the clothes for all the groomsmen. I suppose I was expected to show up on time on the actual day as well. So, I guess I was in charge of two things.

The day before the wedding, at the rehearsal, I passed out all the ties in the shade of cornflower blue to all my grooms-men. I didn't know that was a color until I was told to match it with the bride's maid's dresses. It wasn't until that exact moment, hours before we were supposed to wear them, that I realized I was one tie short. As a dad, chances are you are or were married. So, you know the last thing you want to tell a bride (especially *your* bride) on the eve of her wedding is, "*Honey, we have a problem.*"

The box of cornflower blue ties had been sitting on my kitchen table for weeks. Unopened. It never once crossed my mind to open the box and count the ties just to make sure they were all there. Even after my fiancée asked me (repeat-edly), "*You got everything covered for your guys, right?*" I never opened the box. Now, staring at an empty box that was one cornflower blue tie short, I immediately regretted my lack of ability to provide what was needed.

Nehemiah wouldn't have fallen to the same trouble. He wouldn't have had a mild heart attack in his 20s. No, Nehe-miah thought ahead. He considered all the angles. Had con-tingencies. Nehemiah knew how to solve problems before they became problems. Nehemiah was able to provide for his people when they needed it the most.

Meeting needs

As dads who want to get things right, we can learn from Nehemiah on what it takes to provide for our families. All dads can see the necessity to provide the most basic of needs such as food, shelter, and clothing. But we don't want to be like all other dads. We are called to be set apart. Holy. This means there are other needs that will call for our attention. And we want to be able to provide all the required resources to meet those needs.

So, what do your kids need? Make a list. Think through all the areas of life they need your help to provide for them. Then start attacking those items. Let's start together by examining a few of the ones you and I probably have in common.

Financial provision

Chances are, your nine-year-old doesn't have a job. At least, not one that is going to provide him with the amount of money required to survive. We need to provide for those needs. We need to earn a paycheck. This doesn't mean we have to be *the* provider. You don't have to be the breadwinner in your house or the only one bringing home a paycheck to be a provider for your family. If you married a woman that makes more money than you do, congratulations. You found a winner. But you also have to do your part in providing.

Advice

Our world is full of deceit and evil. There will be no shortage of deception that tries to lead our kids astray. We need to provide helpful advice to assist them in navigating their way down the right path.

Too often, at least when it comes to our kids, we tend to defer to our wives for providing the answers. We neglect to step up and do this ourselves. Raise your hand if you've ever been asked a question from one of your kids and, before you even give it any real thought, you mutter something like, "Go ask your mom." This is simply us pushing our responsibilities onto our partner. Giving her extra obligations. It's a failure to provide on our part.

One of the chief means of provisions should come through leadership. We need to be the ones who teach our sons what kind of men they need to be around girls. How to be respectful. We are the ones who show our daughters the kind of guys they should be looking for in a dating partner.

Safety

As the dad, we must make sure our house is a place of refuge. The outside world can be a place of dangerous uncertainties. And some schools can even seem like they're rougher than prisons. The moment our kids walk inside our homes, they should feel safe. They should know, without a doubt, their dad will do whatever is needed to protect them.

Spiritual leadership

We must guide our children to learn about who God is and how they can know Him. Their spiritual well-being and growth are essential elements in their lives. These are the only areas with eternal value. Because of this, there should be no greater need we look to provide for our kids than strengthening their relationship with their Creator.

How we provide for their spiritual needs says a lot about who we are as dads. It will show them what value we place on discipleship. We need to be heavily involved in teaching them to spend time with God. How to pray. How to read their Bible. How to talk about God and share their faith. We can't let this be a need that goes unmet because we failed to provide.

Provide for times when you're not present

Nehemiah had a life outside rebuilding the wall. He had responsibilities he knew would call him away. At the very least, he knew he wouldn't live forever, so he had to set his people up with a structure that would provide for them when he wasn't around. A parting gift of sorts.

The first thing he did was remove everything from them that was ungodly (Nehemiah 13:30). Their evil practices, harmful relationships, idols, and bad habits. They all had to go. For the people to grow closer to God, Nehemiah had to first remove all the weeds that would strangle that growth.

Next, Nehemiah provided them with a roadmap to accomplish what they needed to do. He gave them duties and responsibilities. He showed them the way. This would provide the people with the ability to do the right thing and make the right choice when Nehemiah was no longer with them. He started them off on the right foot. He even provided the wood that was needed for making offerings and even the first fruits to be offered (Nehemiah 13:31).

One of the best gifts we can provide for our kids is for them to be able to grow in their relationship and follow God without us. We can't be with our kids all the time. We are going to have responsibilities that call us away just as they are going to have their own obligations that will eventually pull them away from home and us. They are going to grow up, move out, and start families of their own. Making sure they start off on the right foot begins now by providing them with a firm foundation to stand upon.

As Nehemiah did, we need to do our best to show them how to remove all that is ungodly and tries to sneak into their lives. We demonstrate spiritual disciplines for them. We help guide them through their relationships while they're young. We warn them of idols. We make them aware of bad habits. We weed the garden.

Doing all these things won't guarantee success. Nehemiah had to return to his people to make corrections (Nehemiah 13). But the people did learn from him. They were better off from his guidance. After doing all he could do for his people, Nehemiah ended his mission the same way he started it, with prayer. At some point, we realize that total control is out of our hands. We have to trust that we have faithfully followed God. He will provide the answers for our kids in all the ways we cannot.

When I came up one cornflower blue tie short, I didn't know what to do. I wasn't the one who provided the solution. My best man's wife grabbed his tie, said, "I'll take care of it," and disappeared into the night. The next morning, she miraculously handed me the extra tie I needed. I didn't ask any questions. Didn't need to. She had provided in ways that I simply couldn't. I like to think I've improved in the ways I provide for my family, but it was definitely a questionable start. When it comes to providing for your family, be like Nehemiah—not me.

CONSIDER THESE QUESTIONS

- Which needs are you doing a good job of providing for when it comes to your family? Which ones could you do a better job of meeting?

- How are you preparing your kids to face the world on their own? What more can you do to help them feel confident in their own choices and actions?

- How does the way we provide for our kids teach them about the way God provides for His children?

8

BY ERIC

The Godly Dad **GLORIFIES** God in All He Does

"And because the gracious hand of my God was on me, the king granted my requests."

NEHEMIAH 2:8

GROWING UP IN A small town has its limitations. But it also has its advantages. One of these perks is the fact that heavy traffic is never an issue. Because of the lack of cars on the roadways, when I was four or five years old, my dad would often let me sit in his lap and "drive" his truck. It made me feel so grown-up.

After each one of my driving experiences, I'd run into the house and brag to my mom about my accomplishments. "I drove us home from the store, Mom. All by myself!" Clearly, I wasn't the brightest of little boys. It wasn't until much later that I understood the truth. I may have been partially sitting in the driver seat, but my father was the one in control. He was the one driving the truck. I was still pretty much just along for the ride.

As dads, we know what our role is supposed to be. We are the leaders of the family. God Himself established this position we are all meant to fill, and we are grateful for the opportunity. Our leadership assignment is one that brings us pride. Unfortunately, there are times we may take a little too much credit for how our family is doing. Like me driving in my dad's lap, we may think we are doing a lot more than we actually are.

So far, in Nehemiah's story, things are going his way. He has this calling to help out his people in Jerusalem. Instead of facing the uncomfortable, possibly dangerous situation of bringing up the conversation before King Artaxerxes, the king asked Nehemiah about his issue (Nehemiah 2:2). Not only does the king start the conversation, he even asked Nehemiah what he wanted to do about his circumstances. Then, the king granted Nehemiah an extended leave of absence to go back and take care of the problems in his homeland. The king also gave Nehemiah letters needed to provide him with safe passage during his travels as well as a king's request for resources required to rebuild the wall. That's a pretty good day in the presence of the king! And Nehemiah knew it wasn't his doing.

God's good hand

Nehemiah was a wise, and godly man. A humble man. He knew the truth of what was going on in his life. It wasn't his charm, cunning words, or personal brilliance which granted him this unbelievable favor with King Artaxerxes. Nehemiah knew immediately that his success came because, "the good hand of my God was upon me" (v2:8). He didn't try for even one second to take the credit for God's work. But we do.

When things in our family are going well, when our little tribe is "succeeding," as the designated chief, we are quick to take credit for the family's prosperity. Even if it is just in our minds, we think, *Look at the excellent job I'm doing!*" But like Nehemiah before the king, our success, every last bit of it, comes from the hand of our good, Heavenly Father. "Every good and perfect gift is from above, coming down from the Father of heavenly lights, who does not change like shifting shadows" (James 1:17). *Every* good gift.

My firstborn daughter is practically perfect. I'm not saying she's a really good girl or that she tries her best. No. I'm saying she is almost perfect. She is respectful. Obedient. Always tries to do the right thing. And she has always been this way. Because of this, my wife and I thought we were the world's greatest parents. We'd take our daughter out to eat and arrogantly shake our heads at parents who had a table full of kids being crazy while our girl was sitting in her seat and eating her food like she was a small adult. *We should give that other family some advice. Help them out. Those parents would probably benefit and love to hear from us.* We even toyed with the idea of teaching a class or writing a book to help the world of struggling parents. THEN, our second daughter was born. All of a sudden, we realized we are not perfect parents. We obviously have no idea what we are doing. We had no business taking credit for how well-behaved our first daughter turned out. Apparently, that was all because the good hand of our God was upon us.

And it's not just our family's behavior, respect, or obedience we dads can take credit for. When the finances are going well—everyone has food to eat, clothes to wear, a nice house to live in, the latest gadgets to entertain them, cars to drive, and nice vacations in the summer—that's because good ole dad is a hard worker. We're good at our job, so we can provide in a good way. Not so fast.

Praise for His provisions

We can provide for our families because God provides for us. When God led His people out of the bondage of slavery they lived through in Egypt, He provided for their every need while they passed through the desert. He gave them food from the sky. Water from rocks. Shade from a pillar of cloud. And even light during the night from a pillar of fire.

Knowing that man has always had an issue taking undeserved credit for gifts they didn't deserve, he told the people

64 | ERIC BALLARD

to be careful to remember exactly who it was that provided and cared for their needs. "He led you through the vast and dreadful wilderness, that thirsty and waterless land, with its venomous snakes and scorpions. He brought you water out of hard rock. He gave you manna to eat in the wilderness, something your ancestors had never known, to humble and test you so that in the end it might go well with you. You may say to yourself, 'My power and the strength of my hands have produced this wealth for me.' But remember the Lord your God, for it is he who gives you the ability to produce wealth" (Deuteronomy 8:15-18).

We tend to only go to God during times of crisis. When things are going bad, we are quick to hit our knees and cry out for help. But when things are going well, when everything seems to be going the way we want with our families, our communication with God takes a bit of a hiatus. What we must realize is that the good times we have are not from the works of our own hands. Not even close. Our success, all of it, is because of the good hand of our good Father. And that truth should lead us to praise His great name.

Thanking God and giving thanks to Him for the work He does in our lives will help us focus the credit for our good where it belongs. It will help eliminate a false sense of pride. It will bring about a grateful heart within us. And it will teach our kids how to praise the God we love and follow. This is the work of a good father.

Passing down the praise

In Genesis 4:1-2, we see the first boys, Cain and Abel, were born. In verse four of the same chapter, we see that the two brothers were each bringing an offering to the LORD. Where did they learn how to do this? Where did they learn how to praise God? Adam must have taught them. They probably saw their father bring offerings to God when they were little. And, chances are, as they grew, Adam explained what he was doing and why he was doing it. The fact that the Bible mentions the boys' bringing a gift to God *one* verse after they were born could imply that Adam treated giving thanks to the glory of God as a high priority. Do we?

One of the best ways we can teach our kids about giving thanks to God and praising His name is by demonstrating it in front of them. This can be done in simple ways. No need to build an altar in the back yard.

When we are telling the family about the promotion we got at work, we should also take a minute to pray as a family thanking God for His provision. We should offer a prayer of thanks before we eat. When we are at church, we should be actively involved in the worship service. Let our kids see us sing along to the praise songs. Let them see us open our Bibles and read along when it comes time for the message. Let's take advantage of these small moments of opportunities to teach our kids about the importance of praising God for all He provides. They can have huge impacts.

- What gift has God given you that you most thankful for? When's the last time you thanked Him for it?

- How can you show your family that all they have is because of how good God has been to them? What can you do to model a heart that beats to praise God?

- It's easy to praise God in the good times. What are some things you can praise Him for during the not-so-good times?

9

BY ERIC

The Godly Dad **RISKS** Comfort to Pursue Calling

"So I went..."

NEHEMIAH 2:9

SEVERAL MONTHS BACK, MY wife and I went on a weekend adventure to celebrate our wedding anniversary. One of our stops was to Inks Lake state park in Burnet, TX. One of the lake's many fingers stretches into a canyon of cut-away rock, creating cliffs on both sides. Many people flock to this natural swimming hole to cliff jump. I was no different.

As I was climbing the final boulder to the highest point of the cliff (maybe 30 feet), I asked the teenager behind me for any tips since this was my first time to Inks Lake. "Jump more to the left," was all he could muster. *Cool. Thanks, guy. Most helpful.* I climbed up the final couple of feet and started to jump. With one foot in the air and most of my momentum moving forward off the cliff, the same teenage guy chimed in, "Be sure to jump far."

It was too late. I was already in the air. And I did not, in fact, jump far. At least not far enough. Soon after I hit the water, I slammed into a boulder below the surface. Luckily, I didn't dive. The only damage was a couple of smashed feet and a banged-up elbow. The mark on the elbow has a big scar. At least I have a cool story.

All scars have stories. Many of them come from adventure—a risk taken. Whether good or bad, we were doing something that spiked our adrenaline, and we got a little scraped up along the way. They leave us with great stories. And these adventure stories tell *our story.*

Risk management

Our teenage years and early twenties are filled with adventures. But as we get older, we tend to become more domesticated. We begin to play it safe. Stick to the sidelines. And I get it. As we mature, we become wiser. We recognize and understand the consequences of danger more fully. We also have more to lose as we get older, which means the stakes are higher. This is where wisdom and maturity come to our aid. These traits that only come with age will keep us from foolish risks. Not all risks are worth taking.

If you're about to do something that feels a bit risky after saying something like, "*Hey man, hold my beer,*" maybe don't do it. Take a pass on that one. While jumping from those boulders was exciting in the moment, crashing into the rocks below the surface was a bit of a wakeup call. It forced some real questions. *If a risk only provides a momentary reward (and only for me), is it worth taking?* It's okay to take a pass on some risks. But let's not pass on all risks. Instead, let's learn to recognize the difference between the *pointless and prideful* risks and the *missional and godly* kind.

If we give up on all risks in the name of playing it safe, we give up on a full life. This full life only comes from following Jesus. Take a small glance through the gospels. Every day with Jesus was an adventure. And a risky one. Miracle healings. Demon confrontation. Push back from the religious leaders. Continuous threats coming from many directions. The same people who praised Jesus one minute were trying to push him off a cliff minutes later (Luke 4:29). Following Jesus was a risk, but faith is risk in action.

Take the leap

In chapter two of Nehemiah, he had made all the arrangements needed to go back home and begin the renovations of Jerusalem. He'd squared everything away with King Artaxerxes. Letters of preparations and resource gathering had been collected. Nehemiah was as ready as he could be. All that was left…was to leave. To take a risk. To go. "So I went…"

That little phrase in verse nine should not be easily dismissed. Taking that first step is usually the most crucial. There is a well-known Chinese proverb that states, "A journey of a thousand miles begins with a single step." Before we can ever reach anything God has called us to, we first have to decide to go.

Before Isaiah became the great prophet, he first answered God's call of *Who should I send? Who will go out for us?* Isaiah heard the call and decided to go. He responded with *Here I am. Send me.* (Isaiah 6:8) Before David became a great warrior for God's people or ever sat on the throne of Israel, he decided to fight Goliath. When everyone else was afraid to move, David communicated to King Saul, *Don't worry about that Philistine any longer; I'll go fight him.* (1 Samuel 17:32). These great men of the Bible didn't become great until they decided *I'll go*. So they went.

But God didn't ask His followers to do things He wasn't willing to do Himself. Jesus left the comforts of heaven and His Father's throne to step down to earth and become one of us. And to take it a step further, when Jesus began His earthly ministry, He had to leave the safety of His carpenter's shop to do that too. Most of His disciples left everything they knew behind to follow Him. So, yeah, there are risks. But if we never take any risks, our lives will never be more than what they are right now. Our faith doesn't grow until it is tested. Until it leads us to take risks. We will never fully know what we're made of until we are truly challenged. Until we step into the unfamiliar.

To follow God today, we'll have to do what men following God have always done. We will have to take a risk, leave the comfortable, and embrace the unknown. So, how do we do this? Where do we start? Like everything always should, this adventure will begin with prayer.

Before Nehemiah did anything, he talked to God. So should we. Let's ask the LORD to show us what He wants us to do. Where is He calling us? When are we to take that step? Are the risks we are about to take from Him or our own desires? We need to tell God that we are prepared and available for whatever it is He wants us to do. We are ready for the risk. This is us going through Isaiah's *send me* phase.

The risks at home

Next, we can start moving towards areas where we see God working. Join Him in His mission. And this mission should begin with the risks we need to engage in at home. Instead of retreating from the hard conversations with our wives, we step in and share what's really going on in our lives. We tell her about the fears we have. We speak about the areas where we feel inadequate. Places we think we're failing. Admit our contributions to the difficulties in our marriages, then voice our commitment to our vows. Getting everything out in the open can certainly feel risky.

Same with our kids. When they start to ask those difficult questions or bring up tough topics that make us feel awkward, instead of passing them off with the casual, *That's something you need to talk to your mom about*, we talk openly and honestly with them. We share our hearts. We listen. Sometimes our kids just need to know that their dad hears them. Really *hears* them. Stepping in to help navigate our kids through the rapids of teenage waters and all the feelings and hormones that go along with them will be risky. There may not be a scarier animal on earth than a tenth-grade girl.

Maybe the risk we take is passing on that promotion we were just offered at work. The pay increase would be nice, but all the travel or overtime hours involved with the added responsibility would take significant time away from our family. I know it seems risky, almost crazy, to pass on a promotion. After all, our work is how we help provide for our family, right? This type of risk involves us trusting in God, not ourselves, to provide for all our needs. If He provides food for the birds and clothing for flowers, He will undoubtedly take greater care of us (Matthew 6:25-30).

Nehemiah took some significant risks returning home and repairing the walls. He probably got a little banged up along the way. But in doing so, his people were forever changed. For the disciples, following Jesus was a world-changing adventure. And everyone involved got scarred-up. But their lives were never the same afterward. They had been changed forever and for the better. Let's go out and take some risks. Collect some scars. Let's teach our kids to be adventurous. To be untamed. To be rowdy in the best sense of the word.

Let them learn how to live their lives by watching us truly live ours. Be wise, for sure, but be wild as well. Take the risk.

CONSIDER THESE QUESTIONS

- What is the biggest risk God has ever called you to take? How did you respond? How did things turn out in the end?

- What emotional scars have you collected from past risks? How do they play a role in the risks you take today?

- What are some risky conversations you need to have with your wife? Your kids?

10

BY KENT

The Godly Dad **DISCERNS** True Needs around Him

"I had not told anyone what my God had put in my heart to do for Jerusalem."

NEHEMIAH 2:12

HAVE YOU EVER JUMPED to a conclusion only to find out later that you were wrong? No? Really? If you haven't, we would never be friends. Have fun in Perfection Land. All by yourself.

For the rest of us, we've done this. Maybe repeatedly. Daily even.

My family still laughs at stories of when I called it wrong. I've walked into a room with two children, one's crying, and the other is standing there, stupefied. I usually assume the one *not crying* is guilty and start doling out accusations, punishments and restoration advice. "Help him! Can't you see he's crying? What did *you DO*? How did you hurt him?!" Or, I'll hear an argument in the other room and bust in with my expert assessment of who's to blame and how they should make it right.

I'm getting better, but I've often reacted to situations around my house with a "talk first, ask later" approach. It's rarely helpful. Usually, it makes things worse. And, it sets a pathetic example of how to resolve conflict and bring restoration.

Nehemiah was a wise, shrewd and observant guy. He was thorough, and often this trait put him several steps ahead of those he was leading.

Gathering information

People knew when Nehemiah arrived in Jerusalem. They'd heard of King Artaxerxes, and word surely spread that a member of the royal entourage was in town. Two of his enemies heard he'd come to seek the welfare of the people of Israel, and they were angry. Nehemiah wanted to get a full grasp on the situation before an all-out battle broke out between him and these knuckleheads, but time was short. He needed to move quickly to understand his options.

Watch what Nehemiah does after being in Jerusalem three days. In chapter 2 verse 12, it says, "Then I arose in the night, I and a few men with me. And I told no one what my

God had put into my heart to do for Jerusalem. There was no animal with me but the one on which I rode."

He rounds up a small posse, snags a horse, and does a mounted survey around the city. Under the cover of night. He inspects the gates, the wall and the surroundings. Chapter 2 goes on to say, "And the officials did not know where I had gone or what I was doing." He was gathering information before he sprung the plan.

This is so counter to my nature! I often want to tell everyone what I'm going to do before I've gathered all the facts or even begun. I'm often quick to speak and slow to listen, even though that's the precise opposite of what James exhorts me to do (James 1:19-20).

Nehemiah was many things: careful, observant, clever and intentional. He was *discerning*.

In chapter 2, we see Nehemiah discerning with his eyes. He's riding around at night, seeing for himself just how bad things are. He's going to share the plan with the leaders soon, and he wants to have first-hand knowledge of the situation. We can learn from this.

Discerning with your ears

But, perhaps, even more valuable, I want to spend the rest of this chapter encouraging you to learn to discern with another of your senses: hearing.

I believe most dads are horrible at this. We have a disease of the mouth called Talkitis. Sadly, many have a corresponding co-infection in our ears called Hearblock. Put these two together and you get T.H.S. – Talkitis-Hearblock Syndrome. Your two major communication organs are damaged. It's like having heart and lung problems at the same time. This won't end well.

We discern best when we're taking input in, not when spewing it out. Put another way, *to discern is to listen.* Listen with our eyes, our ears, our heart, our minds. Discerning is a posture of intake, not outflow. At the moment we're discerning, we're usually receiving, not giving.

Fortunately, there's a cure for this disease! And, it may surprise you to know, the cure isn't just "become a better listener." Now, most of us would benefit greatly by increasing our capacity to listen. I'm growing in this area and hope you are too. There's a shortcut.

What's the fastest cure to the destructive Talkitis-Hearblock Syndrome? *Ask more questions.*

It's so simple, yet, so profound. Let me state it again and more fully. If you'd like to have better communication and connection with your family, ask more questions. Make fewer statements, declarations and edicts. Instead, master the art of communicating through asking.

My most (and least) favorite subject

I love and hate this topic.

I love it because, truly, it's the holy grail for most dads. Learning to ask better questions will revolutionize your family. It's a lifelong crusade worth taking. It unlocks every door of influence and leadership you want to have with them.

It's the one single life skill that I coach dads (and my boys, my wife, my friends, and myself) on more than any other. It reduces heartburn and increases understanding.

Why do I hate this topic? Because, I get widespread agreement on it.

Huh? Why would widespread agreement frustrate me? Because it lulls us into a sense of, "I agree with him, so I got this." I understand, therefore I do. But odds are, dad, when it comes to asking thoughtful questions, you're not as skilled as you think you are. Maybe you have mastered part of it, but not all of it. You're a question-asking amateur, but you're no hall of famer.

It's one thing to comprehend how Drew Brees reads a defense or finds an open receiver. It's quite another to actually do it. It's the difference between being up in the booth and down on the field. Understanding is not doing.

Questions possess power

Think back (maybe ten minutes ago?) to the last time you and one of your family members had a disagreement or misunderstanding. What might that discussion have sounded like if you'd asked a few clarifying questions? "What do you mean exactly by 'I'll be home later'? What time do you think we expect you? Do you know what happens if you miss curfew?"

Questions hijack your brain.

If I ask you, "How many kids do you have?" right now, you are thinking of a number. You can't help *not* to think of a number. There's a ton of brain science to back me up on this. Google it.

In fact, in 1993 researchers discovered the "mere measurement effect." Just by asking a question, they could affect the likelihood of someone taking a prescribed action. In this study, people were asked only *if* they were going to purchase a new car in the next six months. The question alone increased their odds of buying by 35%.[1]

Questions demand our attention, make us think more deeply, and cause powerful chemical and biological reactions. Questions are the touchstone of connection and communication. Another fun Google? "Questions Jesus asked." The master teacher. He knew how our brains were built, so he asked loads of questions.

In the short time we have together, why don't we try to elevate your questioning game? Maybe a notch or two?

The fastest way I know to do that is through a simple chart. Let's break dads into two major groups: the askers and the tellers. Clearly, we're normally bouncing between these two approaches in any given moment. If you're like most dads, your telling skills are okay, but you need some help becoming a better asker. And, if you have only young kids, trust me, you're going to need this skill when they flip the calendar into those teen years!

---

1   https://www.fastcompany.com/3068341/want-to-know-what-your-brain-does-when-it-hears-a-question

Review the chart below, and then let's wrap up by breaking it down together.

Child's Comment	The Teller Dad	The Asker Dad
"Dad, how do you like my drawing?"	"You know, I used to draw back in the day. I was good, too."	"Wow, beautiful! What made you decide to draw that today?"
"Daddy, I love him!"	"Like heck you do! That boy's a bum!"	"What are a couple things about him you most admire?"
"I got a D on a math test."	"What?! There goes your scholarship, young man."	"Whoa, odd. What do you think led to that?" (thru gritted teeth...)
"Dad, listen to me play this song."	"Sounds good. Great. You'll be a pro one day."	"Nice! Hey, what's your favorite type of music these days?"
"I don't wanna do my chores today."	"Well, you're gonna do them, so get over it."	"Would you like to eat or go hungry today?"

On that last one, I kid, I kid (sort of). Clearly, there are times – many of them – when you need to instruct, rebuke, challenge or inform your children. If you're heading out to church, you don't take a poll, "Hey, service is at eleven today, but what time would each of you feel like leaving?" No. The family bus rolls at 10:30, and you'd better be on it. We cannot spend 100% of our parenting time asking questions. But, for many dads, 100% of our time is spent making statements. That's equally problematic.

Dad, when you ask thoughtful, open-ended and sincere questions, you unlock your powers of discernment. You learn what's on your children's hearts, you value and validate them, and you sometimes just buy yourself a few minutes to cool down in the heat of a discussion.

Aren't questions better than statements? See what I did right there? Oh, and there?

CONSIDER THESE QUESTIONS

- Are you more of an "asker" dad or a "teller" dad? In your discussions with your family, what percent of the time are you in each "mode"?

- Think of a person you know who asks thoughtful questions. How could you learn from their example?

- What's one thing you deeply wished your kids "knew by now"? Whatever that is, what would be a few good questions that could help them unlock this realization?

11

BY ERIC

The Godly Dad **CONNECTS** Others to the Mission

"Come, let us rebuild the wall of Jerusalem..."

NEHEMIAH 2:17

IN THE FIRST LORD of the Rings movie, *The Fellowship of the Ring,* fate has tasked a young Hobbit named Frodo Baggins to be the ring bearer of the One Ring. This ring contains incredible power and is being sought after by unrelenting evil forces. For the safety of civilization, the ring must be destroyed, which can only be done in the fires of Mount Doom where it was forged. A small band of friends joins Frodo as he sets off on this daunting adventure. As their expedition grows increasingly dangerous, Frodo decides to break away from the group to finish his calling on his own. All his companions let him go it alone—all but Sam.

Frodo climbs into a boat and paddles off to begin his solo journey. To his surprise, Sam bursts through the woods, calling out for Frodo to wait. "Go back, Sam. I'm going to Mordor alone," Frodo responds determinedly. "Of course you are," Sam answers back. "And I'm coming with you." Unable to swim, Sam hesitates on the beach for a second. Then he runs into the water, chasing after Frodo. After a few steps into the lake, Sam begins to sink. Frodo had to pull Sam out of the water and into the boat to keep him from drowning. It is only after seeing the unwavering perseverance of his friend that Frodo allows Sam to join him in his mission.

Why do men try to tackle everything on their own? We all do it. Like Frodo, we try to take on these larger-than-life-sized missions by ourselves. A lone wolf. And this mentality starts at a very early age. When your kids were toddlers and trying to prove to you how grownup they were becoming, they probably bragged about their solo accomplishments. "Look, Dad, I tied my shoes. And I did it *all by myself.*" The only difference for some of us is, as we get older, the "shoes" get bigger.

A year or two into my marriage, I attempted a simple remodeling project at home. It did not go well. Noticing my struggles, my wife suggested I call her dad, who happened to be a contractor and ask for some help. *No way!* Like a toddler,

I proudly said, "I can do this *all by myself.*" But I couldn't. After a lot of time and money, I called my father-in-law for guidance. After a quick conversation with him, I understood exactly what I needed to do and how to do it.

The more the merrier

That voice inside of us, pushing us to "go it alone," is leading us astray. This is not how we were created. I was never meant to go it alone or do things *all by myself.* In the very beginning, while Adam worked the garden and took on the task of naming the animals, God looked at man and said, "It is not good for the man to be alone. I will make a helper suitable for him" (Genesis 2:18).

We need help. Regardless of how smart, strong, or capable we may be, we can only do so much on our own. We can only achieve so much by ourselves. If Nehemiah tried to rebuild the walls of Jerusalem all by himself, it would never have happened. He may have gotten off to a good start, but he couldn't have finished it. He understood that. He knew he needed help. So, he went out and began recruiting others. Nehemiah found like-minded people and shared his passion to join his efforts.

As godly dads, we should follow Nehemiah's example and bring people in to support the mission God has placed on our hearts. And the first partner we must include is the one we married. The pride of a husband can drive him to be the one to try to carry all the weight and workload of the marriage. *If I handle all the pressures alone, then she doesn't have to.* While that may be a noble sentiment, it's a faulty approach to marriage. Any relationship where one person does all the work and makes all the decisions without including the other person is not a partnership. It's a dictatorship. Before Nehemiah ever stacked one brick on top of another, he recruited help. He connected people with God's mission. He formed a team.

Wise guys

Like Nehemiah, we need a team of people to help us build up our families. It's essential to find and partner up with people that have the skills we want and need. When I was first married, I started meeting with a man who had been married for decades. He was the kind of godly man who I'm pretty sure had regular face-to-face meetings with the Creator. And from my observations, his marriage was a strong one. We started having lunch 2-3 times a month, in which a majority of the time was spent with me peppering him with questions about how to start a healthy marriage. How to be a good husband. How to lead well. It was an invaluable learning process for me.

A note from the other guy: Pause for a moment. As you know, Eric and I (Kent) co-authored this book. This chapter was written by Eric. I want you to notice something. Re-read the above paragraph. Do you see what Eric did? He "started meeting with" a man who had more knowledge than he did. Did you notice later he said, "...me peppering him with questions..."? I want to make sure you didn't just read past that and think, "Oh, that's a nice thing Eric did. He's so smart." Brother, he's sharing pure gold with you. Don't just skim past it. Get around wiser men and ask them how they became so wise! Okay, that's enough. If I keep going with these compliments for Eric, he'll get a big(ger) head. I now return you to your regularly scheduled broadcast.

I did the same thing when my wife got pregnant the first time. As soon as the doctor told us we were having a girl, I found men in our church who had girls and started spending deliberate time with them. I still do this today. My girls are in elementary school, so I look for men I trust who have daughters in Junior High and ask them questions. What can I expect? How should I handle certain situations? What do you wish you knew before your girls became teenagers? I'm finding mentors so that I can learn from those who have gone before me. To help us become the men, husbands, and fathers we want to be, we need to find the men we want to be like and spend time with them.

It takes mentors

We aren't the only ones who need a team to help us grow and fulfill God's mission in our lives. Our kids need mentors. They need more voices than just ours speaking truth into their lives. I spent nearly two decades serving churches as a youth pastor. During that time, I had a front-row seat to the difference made in the lives of teenagers who had a handful of adults pouring into and investing in their hearts. Our voice should be a resonating note that focuses our kid's hearts on the LORD. But the more voices involved, the more harmonizing the message will be. A sweeter melody.

One night after our student ministry's small group meetings, the mom of a 7th-grade girl stuck around to talk to her daughter's small group leader. This is what she told the girl's leader: *Thank you so much for all you have been doing and teaching my daughter. She comes home every week, talking about what she has learned from you. Most of it sounds a lot like the exact things I've been trying to teach her at home. You know, the ideas she rolls her eyes at and dismisses. What she ignores from me, she hears from you. I'm so grateful that God has sent her another woman to reinforce the ideas we are trying to teach her at home.*

When our kids are young, our words seem to be as good as gospel to them. But as they grow, they will naturally start to search for outside voices to learn from. This is just part of the growth process. We want to make sure that we are doing our best to connect them with the right people. A chorus of godly voices declaring godly messages.

There is still something inside me that wants to accomplish everything on my own. To be a self-made man. But this is not wise. And it is not sustainable for the long haul. Being a dad is a life-long calling. Trying to do it all on my own will cause me to crash and burn way too soon. To be successful, to build the foundational walls of our families, we need to follow Nehemiah's example. We need to recruit others and connect them to this fatherly mission God has called us to follow.

CONSIDER THESE QUESTIONS

- Why do most men try to do things on their own? What is gained from accomplishing something alone?

- Who are some men that have characteristics or qualities you admire? How can you connect with them to learn from their wisdom?

- Who are some mentors you can start trying to line your kids up with? What other voices do they need to hear God's truth from?

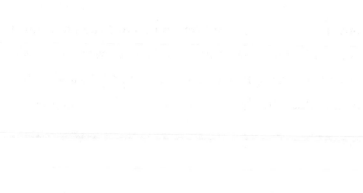

12

BY ERIC

The Godly Dad **FOCUSES** Despite Life's Distractions

"...they mocked and ridiculed us..."

NEHEMIAH 2:19

NEHEMIAH HAD COME A long way. And so far, everything had been working out for him. He had received King Araxerxes' permission and blessing to return to Jerusalem to rebuild the broken-down walls. He had secured safe passage. He had been given the resources needed for all the construction work. And he had been successful in recruiting a team of people in his efforts. Everyone wanted to help rebuild the wall! Well…not everyone. Nehemiah made enemies. Outsiders who chose to criticize and tear down constantly.

You ever seen that old cinematographic masterpiece Christmas special about Rudolph the red-nosed reindeer? It's one of those creepy stop motion Claymation cartoons from the 1960's? By some spectacular congenital anomaly, Rudolph was born with a nose that glows. And when his snout lights up, it makes a sound like a toddler attempting to play the pan flute for the first time. Nails across the chalkboard. This, of course, makes Rudolph stand out. He's different. And he's the only one.

His famous song informs us—since you have kids, I'm sure you've sung it a few times—all the other reindeer used to laugh at Rudolph and call him names. They wouldn't even let him join in any of their reindeer games. They were naysayers. Scoffers. They stood in the way of Rudolph's efforts and mission. Cruel bullies. But when the winter storms threatened to cancel Christmas, who did Santa turn to for salvation? That's right. Rudolph. It can be a difficult thing to push past all the opposition and distractions that come our way, but it can also be the exact thing that saves the day.

While poor Rudolph's story is part fable and fairytale, ours is not. As fathers trying to raise a godly family, we are going to face opposition. Criticism. Distractions. It's going to happen. Not everyone is going to like you or what you are doing. And if they do, you're doing something wrong. In fact, trying to be a godly father nowadays can sometimes make you stick out as much as Rudolph's nose did. But, that's a good thing, my friend.

One Sabbath, while Jesus was teaching, people came from all over to be near Him. To be healed by Him. To touch Him. They all recognized His power and authority. While they were flocking to Jesus, He turned to His disciples and gave them some profound warnings. Among them was this disturbing prediction, "What sorrow awaits you who are praised by the crowds, for their ancestors also praised false prophets" (Luke 6:26).

Because we have chosen to follow the ways of Jesus instead of the ways of the world, it only makes sense we would face opposition and hostility. If the world hated Jesus, it's going to hate us too (John 15:18). Even the people of His day who claimed to be godly and religious were always giving Jesus a hard time.

The same, but different

We swim upstream. This fact alone will lead to resistance. And it will come at us from all areas of our lives.

For example, let's say you're away on a business trip. After the work is done and the sales are made, your coworkers start looking for a way to unwind and celebrate. It's likely the kind of good time they are searching out might not line up with your ideas of a good time. It's decision time now. What do you do? Instead of going out with them, you could go back to your room. Call your wife and kids before bed to celebrate with them. Even though this is the right choice, you'll probably face pushback for making it. *"Come on, man. You want to be part of the team, right? I thought you were one of us!"*

It's incredible how little peer pressure strategies have changed since high school days. But the pressure feels real. Would not going out with them make you look like you're not a team player? Would it have effects on the job opportunities which come your way? The promotion you are working towards?

It's easy for men to give in to this type of opposition. We can even rationalize it as if it's a good thing. *I'm only doing this to keep my job. I need my job to provide for my family. So, in a way, I'm doing this for my family.* If you ever think going down the wrong path is done in the name of your family, you're fooling yourself.

Most bosses who have any real authority don't care how you celebrate your job. They care if you are a valuable employee. A hard worker. They are searching for men they can trust. Men of integrity. And saying "no" when everyone around you is saying "yes" is a great way to set yourself apart from the crowd. It's possible making the right choice just might be what gives you the advantage you've been looking for.

Observe how Nehemiah dealt with opposition. He told everyone about the experiences he had with the king and his journey to Jerusalem. He reminded them of their circumstances, then revealed his plans to rebuild the walls. Most people were all for it, but there were a handful of individuals who scoffed at Nehemiah's intentions. His response was simple. "The God of heaven will help us succeed. We, his servants, will start rebuilding this wall" (Nehemiah 2:20). He let the words of his opposition roll right off his back. He batted away their distractions like a hanging curveball and refocused his team and his efforts. *We are going to rebuild this wall. God will make it a success.* 'Atta boy, Nehemiah. *That's* how you face opposition.

Pushing past the distractions

You and I don't need to prepare ourselves just in case voices of distraction come our way. What we need to prepare ourselves for is how we are going to respond to the naysayers and other voices of distraction when they come our way. Because they're coming. Not if, but when. Both Peter and John made mention of not being surprised about the opposition and struggles that are going to come our way (1 Peter 4:12, 1 John 3:13). Enemies only attack threats. When we follow Jesus, we become a threat to the enemy. The closer we follow Jesus, the more of a threat we become. The more opposition is bound to be thrown our way. The size of our opposition is often proportionate to our endeavor. Paul, possibly the greatest example of a Christ-follower, said, "a great door for effective work has opened to me, and there are many who oppose me" (1 Corinthians 16:9).

Nehemiah's mission was at the forefront of his mind. Always. It was his priority. He was able to stay focused and on track because his priorities were clear. Anything that got in the way of his God-given goals was ignored, especially the clamoring of the naysayers. We must do the same.

Take a minute and write down your top five priorities. Don't overthink this; just write down the first five things that pop in your mind. Regardless of how you prioritize your different tasks, goals, and objectives, there will be people and activities that fight to distract you. We have to be able to focus on what's important and ignore what's not.

What we need to learn from this little priority setting exercise is not that all distractions come from bad places. College football is one of the great gifts that God has given to mankind. It's fantastic. But, if you spend all day Saturday watching college football and then chase it down with a Sunday spent on the couch watching NFL games, you are letting football distract you from your priorities. Golf is not an evil game (except when I play it). But if you spend five or six hours every weekend on the course, you're being distracted from more important matters. If you're a dad with kids still living in your home and your golf handicap is going *down* – and you're not out on the PGA Tour – there's probably an issue.

As Nehemiah started his journey to Jerusalem, he possibly practiced the speeches he would make once he arrived. How he would rally the people together. What he would say. How he should say it. It's also possible he prepared for how he would handle the opposition. Strategies he would use to maintain focus among such distractions. This would have allowed him to push aside the naysayers trying to derail his message so easily. His focus maintained his determination. As godly dads, we carry around some significant priorities. Stay focused. Stay determined. Push away the distractions. As we carry out every one of those steps, we will take steps closer to the goal.

CONSIDER THESE QUESTIONS

- What's the best way you know to focus in on God and His leading? How do you put this strategy into practice?

- What are some signals that show you are being distracted from God-oriented goals? What can you do to eliminate these distractions?

- Who are the biggest naysayers in your life? What do you think is the best way to respond to them?

13

BY ERIC

The Godly Dad **MOBILIZES** People to Use Their Gifts

"Eliashib the high priest and his fellow priests went to work and rebuilt the Sheep Gate..."

NEHEMIAH 3:1

MY FIRST JOB WAS in construction. The summer I turned sixteen, I headed out to a job site to learn how to build houses. Or so I thought. What I actually did was move the scaffolding. Pick up trash. Carry wood from one place to another. Lay roofing felt under a sizzling southern summer sun. You know, the fun stuff no one else wanted to do. Even though my role on the crew was at the bottom and my skill set next to nothing, I was still part of the crew. I contributed. I worked. I did my part. And for years afterward, every time I drove past that home I worked on when I was a teenager, I would tell whoever was in the car, "I helped build that house right there."

As Nehemiah led the rebuilding of Jerusalem's walls, he mobilized the people by assigning everyone specific tasks. Each person involved in the project was – actually – *involved* in the project. No one sat on the sidelines. Not only did everybody know what the plans for the rebuild were, they knew how their piece of work fit into the scheme. This gave them ownership. A sense of pride that drove them to do their best. The wall was *theirs*. Every time they walked past their section, they told the people next to them, "I helped build that wall."

As we lead the growth and development of our families, one of our ongoing tasks is to make sure everyone in the family knows they are part of the family. A vital part. There's a big difference between people living under the same roof and people being part of a family. It's our job as a husband and father to ensure everyone in our family knows the role they play. To do this, we, like Nehemiah, have to mobilize our people into being active participants of the family. No one sits on the sidelines.

Focusing on the mission

Before we begin passing out assignments, we must have an overarching purpose or mission for our family. What is the overall goal we are trying to achieve? Nehemiah was building

102 | ERIC BALLARD

a wall. He made his plans and strategies known to the people. Everyone knew what the mission was.

What are we building? A family focused on prayer? One concentrated on generosity? Maybe you want your family to be service or missions oriented. Whichever direction you feel God is leading your family, make sure they all know what direction that is. Let it be a phrase you repeat over and over. Maybe you write out a tagline and emblazon it on a family crest. Cross-stitch it into every pillow in your house if you have to. Do whatever must be done to ensure everyone is clear on what the family stands for.

Once the mission is clear, it's time for mobilization. Everyone needs a role and an assignment. Being actively involved drives buy-in. The size of the role isn't the primary goal. Ownership is. They need to be a contributor and realize the value of their contribution. Our kids need to know that their job is significant. That we, as a family, are all pulling in the same direction, and their efforts help move us all along. If anyone isn't doing their part, our family won't be as strong as it could be. Their part is vital.

When a good friend of mine was in second or third grade, his dad drove a food delivery truck. He would drive around to the local restaurants and shops to drop off their supplies for the day. In the summers, my friend would ride around with his dad and help drop off some of the easier deliveries. When the managers and owners of the shops saw my friend, they would comment to his dad, "I see you brought a helper today." He told me that his dad's response was always the same, "This is my right-hand man. I couldn't get this job done without him."

As my friend retold this story for me, it was obvious he was playing the events of those past years over again in his mind. A smile crept across his face as the memories came rushing back. I couldn't help but notice; here we were some four decades later, and he was detailing times his dad made him feel as though he played a vital role. Every time we bring our kids into the mission, we're creating memories they may relay many years from now. It's important.

Talents and gifts

Before we move any further, let's be clear on our terminology. When we speak about *talents or abilities*, we're talking about a natural skill that is passed down through DNA and perhaps enhanced through practice and hard work. Hitting a baseball or solving equations, for example. When we talk about *gifts*, we are referring to spiritual gifts given to us by the Holy Spirit to bless others and glorify God's name. An example of this could be the way your kid is great at making new people feel welcomed into her friend group, demonstrating her gift of compassion. Both are important to recognize and encourage. But only one has eternal value, so let's be sure we are enforcing those gifts as much as possible.

As the ones leading the charge, we need to learn how to tie our kids' talents into the roles they play in the family. If you have one kid who is showing an ability with numbers, bring him into the process of planning the family vacation. Let him help out on how the money will be spent. How much of the budget goes towards the place you stay? Food? Activities? Souvenirs? Maybe you have a kid that never stops taking pictures with her phone. She becomes the memory-maker. She's the one responsible for getting the family photos during the holidays, vacations, graduations, and other life events.

To give tasks to our kids that are fitting to their spiritual gifts, we have to know what their gifts are. Pay attention to how they are gifted. How they are unique. Then we support that gifting through encouragement and providing opportunities to practice and further develop that gift. If you have a kid that looks to be servant-hearted, let him plan out a service project for the family to take part in. If one kid is displaying the gift of being peaceable, let her voice her thoughts when arguments arise in the family.

Compliment, don't compare

Even though you know this, I'm going to say it anyway. Your kids are different from each other. They are not the same. We must validate their different abilities differently. We shouldn't compare them to each other or say, "Why can't you be more like your sister?!" This rarely works as a motivator or encouragement. In most cases, the opposite is true. Comparisons and comments like that tend to make kids want to give up, not try harder.

School came pretty easy to me. Then again, I grew up in Mississippi, and our track record in the arena of education isn't the best. Either way, I made pretty good grades with little effort. But school was more of a struggle for my younger sister. Often, when she had a teacher in school that I previously had, she'd eventually have a comparison leveled at her that was a negative dig. It never made her work harder in school. It just made her dislike the teacher more.

Depending on how different your kids are from one another, chances are they will probably hear the comparisons outside the home. Don't make them listen to it inside as well. Allow and encourage them to use their different skill sets and gifts in different ways.

Just because our kids are talented in certain areas doesn't mean they don't have to help out in other areas. They have to learn that we don't just do the jobs we are good at or like to do. Not everyone building the wall with Nehemiah was a skilled carpenter or abled mason. They were district rulers, priests, merchants, goldsmiths, perfume-makers, and countless other professionals. Despite them being proficient in other areas, many jobs needed to be done for the betterment of the whole group. So, everyone rolled up their sleeves and got to work. This often included doing some jobs that no one else wanted to do. It is unlikely that anyone "volunteered" to repair the dung gate, but it was a job that had to be done, so someone did it. Even if your son isn't "talented" at taking out the trash, he can do it as a way of meeting a vital family need.

I bet once the final brick was placed and the walls were finished, everyone involved grew closer to one another. They became a family of sorts. By giving our kids a mission they understand and an important role in that mission, our family will be stronger.

- What do you feel God is leading your family to do? What's the mission? How does He want your family to be defined?

- What are some of your kids' talents? What are some of their gifts? What do you do to encourage both in their lives?

- How do you involve your kids in the family mission? How do you incorporate their talents and gifts into making the family stronger?

14

BY ERIC

The Godly Dad **INTERCEDES** on Behalf of His Family

"Hear us, our God, for we are despised..."

NEHEMIAH 4:4

WHEN IT CAME TIME for me to get a new computer, I headed down to the Apple store and picked out a laptop. When I told one of the sales associates, a red-shirted guy from their *Genius Bar*, what computer I wanted, he asked me, "Why are you going to buy that one?" Now, I wasn't ready for follow-up questions, plus it seemed like a weird approach to sales, right? *You want to buy our product? Why?* Ill-prepared for his question, I just answered, "Work."

He responded with another question, "What kind of work are you going to use it for?" *Seriously, dude!* Seeing the blank stare on my face, the guy went into a long spill of technical jargon about the computer's specs. Something about quad-core-megabytes, retina-display-inputs, and flux-capacitors. I didn't understand a word of it.

While he was still talking, I turned around and walked out of the store. I needed someone to intercede for me. Someone that could speak a tech language I didn't understand. Standing outside the Apple store, I called my wife—she has a Ph.D. in Industrial Engineering and is crazy smart. When she answered the phone, I said, "I need you to come and talk to a guy about a computer for me." A true story that I am only a little ashamed of.

Out of all the spiritual disciplines, I believe prayer is one of the most difficult. Possibly *the* most difficult. It's like when I was in the Apple store. Sometimes, prayer seems like a language I'm struggling to pick up. I know that sounds odd considering prayer is simply communicating with God.

Think about your own prayer life for a minute. Does it come naturally to you or is it a challenge? If you could dial your prayer life up, what would that be worth to you?

The power of prayer

In the book of Daniel, King Darius is tricked into making it illegal to pray to any other god besides himself for 30 days. He made prayer (to other gods) a capital offense. When Daniel heard about the new law, he responded by going to his regular place of prayer to pray. He prayed three times a day, giving thanks to the LORD, just as he had always done before (Daniel 6:10).

Let's say I told you, "If you pray in the next 30 days, you'll be tossed into a pit of hungry lions," what would your response be? Would you think *You know, it's worth the risk* or more like *I could probably wait a month*? If you're like me, this kind of choice is a no brainer. I'd take the month of silence with God. But not Daniel. To him, prayer was like breathing. If he couldn't do it, he was already dead. It appears that Daniel believed nothing could be done without somehow involving prayer.

Nehemiah was a man of the same beliefs. If you look at the book of Nehemiah as a whole, a consistent theme running through the words of every chapter is Nehemiah interceding for his people. And he did it through prayer.

When Nehemiah originally heard the news of the state of his hometown, the first thing he did was hit his knees in prayer. For days, he interceded for his people before his God (Nehemiah 1:4). And this wasn't a one-time thing. Throughout his book, Nehemiah was continuously speaking to the LORD on his people's behalf.

As a dad, there may not be an activity that more positively impacts your children than your praying for them. Nothing has the potential of having a powerful impact the way prayer does. Again, this begs the question, what's your prayer life worth to you? Or, perhaps, the real question is, what's your prayer life worth to *your wife and kids?*

Prayer in the life of dads

As we were leaving the hospital with our first-born child, I tried to impress on the medical staff how irresponsible it was for them to trust my wife and me with the life of another human. Despite my protests, they assured me we'd be fine. It took us about two hours to drive the seven miles back to our house. There was no traffic, I just made sure the speedometer never elevated above the lightning-quick pace of 10 miles per hour. I even sat through some traffic signals a couple of times, *just to be extra cautious.*

That first night we put our baby girl to bed, I snuck into her room after she was asleep and prayed for her. Her whole life was a book full of blank pages, and I knew prayer was the best way I could help her write her story. I continued this spy-like routine of praying for my daughter night after night for weeks. It was intentional. Vital. Something that had to be done. Then, all of a sudden and without reason, I stopped. Something so crucial in the beginning became casual. *Why? What happened?*

My story is the same as that of dads all over the world. It may sound a lot like yours. We start with the best of intentions. Then, for reasons we can't even put our finger on, we stop. We sort of take the approach of hoping for the best while simply letting things play themselves out. Nehemiah was more intentional with his mission. He intervened on his peoples' behalf every chance he got, lifting them up in prayer. We must follow his example and be dads who pray for our people. Our wives. Our children.

I know that prayer is essentially the act of talking to and listening to God. But what makes prayer so powerful is not *what* we are doing but *Who* we are doing it with. If you are a godly man – and since you're reading this book, chances are good that you are – then you believe that when you pray, you are speaking directly to the Creator of the universe. Not only that, you believe this God actually hears you when you speak to Him. You believe *God listens to you* when you talk to Him. This is an incredible truth. One we need to pass down to our kids.

Passing down prayer

Because it is an incredible gift that is difficult to understand fully, prayer is something we should spend significant time teaching our kids to do. This will start by praying *with* them. They will learn to talk to God by watching and listening to us pray.

For years, when I was younger, I would pray by resting my head on a balled-up fist like the sculpture *The Thinker*. The reason I did this was because that's how I saw my dad pray when we said the blessing at the dinner table. Kids learn by watching. But *teaching* our kids to pray will take more than just praying *with* them.

After following Jesus for a while, the disciples picked up on the fact that the way they prayed to God seemed to be different than the way Jesus did it. So, they asked for help. "Lord, teach us to pray" (Luke 11:1). In response, Jesus gave them a simple framework of prayer to work with. Then he gave them storied examples of right and wrong ways to pray (Luke 11:1-13 and Matthew 6:5-15). Maybe your kids will ask you to teach them to pray. Maybe they won't. Either way, it should be a habit you do your best to pass on to them.

Explain to them everything you know about prayer. You don't have to have all the answers to their every question. Just break down the how's and why's of your prayer life. Maybe walk them through the template Jesus provided for His disciples in the Lord's prayer. Tell them to start by praising the name of God. Then ask for His guidance. Ask for His provisions for their needs. Seek His forgiveness and the ability to forgive others. Keeping it simple should help them embrace it more easily.

We will never be able to control the prayer life of our kids. But we can control our prayer life *for* our kids. We should lift them up before the King of kings regularly. The first words off our lips should be for their salvation. Their meeting and knowing Jesus as soon as possible will impact their whole life. And the life to come. Then we should pray for God to send them godly friends.

As a veteran youth pastor, I've seen first-hand how a teenager's friends can lead them in two very different directions. We should pray for our kids' futures. The choices they will make. The paths they will take. It's never too early to pray for their future spouse. We should also pray for the challenges they will face. The struggles your kids will face will be similar, while at the same time vastly different than the challenges you faced at their age. Pray for them when you are at odds with each other. Pray when you're mad or disappointed in them. There is no bad time or way to pray for your kids. Interceding for them before the God that formed them is one of our primary responsibilities as fathers.

If you are looking for more ways to pray for your kids, simply ask them. Deliberately asking your kids for specific ways you can pray for them will open so many doors of conversations and opportunities for the two of you to grow closer. Simply put, pray for your kids. It will change their lives and yours.

CONSIDER THESE QUESTIONS

- What do you think God does when you intercede for your kids with prayer? How do you think your prayers affect the lives of your kids? Does this make you want to pray more or less for your family? Why?

- How have you tried to teach your kids to pray? Do they see prayer as a priority of yours? Why or why not?

- What are some simple steps you could take to help prayer be something you and your kids do regularly?

15

The Godly Dad **PROTECTS** Loved Ones from Danger

"They all plotted together to come and fight against Jerusalem and stir up trouble against it."

NEHEMIAH 4:8

DURING MY SENIOR YEAR of high school, we were playing one of our competitive rivals in a crucial soccer game to determine which team would advance to the playoffs. There were years of conflict between the two teams. Even before the kickoff, tensions were high. Every interaction on the field was a heated one. Dirty tackles. Cheap shots when the refs weren't looking. Lots of trash talk. As the end of the second half was fast approaching, things escalated.

While battling for the ball, I grabbed one of their players and threw him to the ground. Understandably, his teammates had a problem with my actions, and four of them came running at me to retaliate. Then, just as they reached me, they stopped and slowly backed away. Confused by their sudden halt, I looked around to figure out what was going on. That's when I felt his hand on my shoulder. Kyle, our back-up goalkeeper. He was a mountain of a man. The biggest and strongest guy I have ever personally known. When he saw the other team running at me, he stepped off the bench and simply stood behind me. Arms folded. *Don't do it* written across his face. Just the sight of him was enough to send the other team in the opposite direction. Under Kyle's protection, I was kept safe.

Nehemiah's wall-building project was starting to take shape. Because of the people's enthusiastic efforts, the wall had been rebuilt to half its original height. They had reached the midway point in no time. All the naysayers were no longer satisfied by tearing down the wall with just their words. They were planning an actual attack. One that would bring real harm to Nehemiah and his people. As Kyle did for me, Nehemiah was determined to protect his people.

A call to arms

Do not be deceived. We are in a real battle. We have an undeniable enemy. And his attacks are evident. As dads, our job is that of protector. We are posted to stand on the wall and keep watch. We must sound the alarm and raise the warning flag when we see trouble approaching on the horizon. And when the fight reaches our front door, we take action.

There is just so much evil in the world, it's hard even to know where to begin our preparations in protecting our family. It starts by making them aware of possible threats. Nehemiah didn't give up the mission when danger started to rear its ugly head. There was no hiding. Nehemiah told his people about the dangers that loomed out in the distances. Then he put swords in their hands.

Be honest with your kids about the dangers that linger about in their schools, the places they hang out, the people they'll encounter. Help them be aware of their vulnerability to online predators. Then equip them with the weapons they need to defend themselves. Put a sword in their hands.

If our kids are ignorant to the possible perils they'll face, there's a good chance they'll stumble into the pitfalls. If they are unaware that the people they go out with won't always have the purest of intentions, they can end up in dangerous situations. If they don't know what trouble can look like, they may not recognize it when they see it.

Obviously, we need to be careful and age-appropriate in this. Our six-year-olds probably don't need to understand the reason *why* they shouldn't take candy or get into cars with strangers. They just need to know not to do it. But when they are teenagers, understanding the *why* gives them a clearer picture of the enemy they are up against. We must make sure they are informed about the risks out there and the individuals who might prey on them. They should learn from us about the dangers that can arise on dates, in the classroom, at mass gathering events, or even while they're browsing through their feeds on social media.

Don't lock them in their rooms and hide them away from the world. Instead, put a sword in their hand. Show them how to protect themselves in all those future moments when you won't be around to fight for them.

Sharper than any double-edged sword

One of the best ways we can arm our kids to protect themselves is with sound doctrine. Give them a right and deep understanding of God's word. When their friends tell them the clothes they wear and the way they look are the most important things, they'll know *that's not what the Bible says.* When they are pushed into thinking that physical expressions of romantic feelings are the best way to show someone you care about them, they'll know that's wrong because the Bible details what real love looks like. When few people "like" their posts, pics, or comment in hateful ways to make them feel bad about themselves, they'll know the God who formed them with His own hands has gone to great lengths to declare in His Word how loved they are.

Giving our kids a clear picture of Jesus and His Word will help them see everything else more clearly as well. Nehemiah told his people, "Don't be afraid of the enemy! Remember the

Lord, who is great and glorious," (Nehemiah 4:14). Being able to remember God and His Word in times of enemy attacks will equip our kids to fend off the adversary's assaults.

While making our kids aware of possible threats and giving them strategies to protect themselves, sometimes you still have to clear the temple. Early in His ministry, Jesus and His disciples made their way to Jerusalem during the Passover holiday. When Jesus entered the temple courts, He witnessed a scene that was simply unacceptable. Swindlers taking advantage of people from out of town. Thugs cheating people at their money exchange tables. They had taken God's house and turned it into a for-profit marketplace.

Jesus couldn't sit idly by and let this continue. He flipped over the tables of these crooked moneychangers. He drove their inventory of cattle out with a whip. He demanded everyone make a quick exit. The disciples watched in shock and awe while Jesus picked a fight with an entire gang of goons all on His own. They saw Jesus actively protecting the people from being confused about the true nature and purpose of God's House.

It's important to note while Jesus was angry and took physical action, He wasn't out of control. He wasn't *reacting* out of rage. He was in control. He knew what He was doing. After seeing the mockery these delinquents were making of His Father's house, Jesus didn't explode on them. This was an act of protection, not vindication. He walked out of the temple and made a whip (John 2:15). The time it took to make his whip would have given Him an opportunity to collect His thoughts. Gather the right plan of attack. Yet, He still attacked. He went after the threat.

Let me be clear. I don't think we should go out looking for fights. It is probably best to walk away from almost all altercations. But when it comes to protecting our families, if a fight is needed, rolling up our sleeves so we can better throw a punch is not a bad idea. The Bible is full of people defending their families and people. Abraham rescued Lot (Genesis 14). David took down a giant (1 Samuel 17). Nehemiah cracked some heads (Nehemiah 13:25). And Jesus cleared the temple.

Not a fight of flesh and blood

In the Old Testament, God called men like Abraham, David, and Nehemiah into physical altercations to protect His people. More than likely, this will not be the case for us. Our "fights" will probably be those of a more spiritual nature. Battling to protect the minds of our kids while teaching them how to make wise choices. Wrestling with the poor influences that clamor for our kids' attention. Going into combat against the dangers hiding online in social media or those embedded in the craziness of our culture. Our crusade may not be physical, but spiritual warfare is just nonetheless real.

To protect our kids, we need to prepare them for battle. They need to know how the enemy attacks. They need to understand how to sidestep all the dangers that come after them. But there will be times they come across battles that are bigger than they are. They won't be able to defend themselves

122 | ERIC BALLARD

effectively. As their loving father, we must step in and fight for them in ways they cannot. To protect us from sin and death, our Heavenly Father fought for us in ways we couldn't. Jesus came to earth and tackled problems that were beyond our own ability to solve. His fight was a bloody one. And His victory was our victory. He went to the greatest lengths imaginable to protect His people. We should do the same.

CONSIDER THESE QUESTIONS

- What is the most significant danger threatening your kids right now? How are you helping them fight against it?
- What are some "weapons" you can arm your kids with to give them confidence against the enemy?
- What role does God play in helping you protect your family?

16

BY ERIC

The Godly Dad
RECONCILES People
with Wise Counsel

"When I heard their outcry and these charges, I was very angry."

NEHEMIAH 5:6

AS CAN HAPPEN WITH every ongoing relationship, eventually people begin to get on each other's nerves. Tensions rise, and quirky habits that once seemed amusing become the most annoying thing in the world. All relationships – all of them – will go through rough patches. Careless words are tossed about. Spiteful actions that normally never show up now suddenly appear. Because relationships form between people, and people can be – well, people – we aren't always going to get along all the time. It just won't happen.

When I was a senior in high school, one of my best friends and I were heading off to different colleges. We had always gotten along great with no fighting. But a couple of months before we were to leave for our different schools, we began to fight all the time. And we really couldn't even tell you what it was about. It was just fighting.

I talked to my youth pastor about it, and he responded with, "Oh, yeah. Happens all the time." I asked *what* happens all the time? He told me it was common for close friends who were about to head off in different directions to fight about anything and everything. He said it was a subconscious way of people trying to make their split from each other an easier one. Once I understood what he was talking about, I could see it when I was hanging out with my friend. My youth pastor had helped me reconcile things. My friend and I didn't fight after that. It was once again like it had always been with him.

A common point of reference

The weight of the wall rebuild was starting to bubble to the surface. The continuous stress of the project and daily challenges were becoming too much for the people to bear. Times were tough, and the circumstances were causing people to act in ways they usually wouldn't. They began to turn on each other and became rude and selfish. Nehemiah heard the complaints of his people and became angry. Everyone was on the same team. Part of the same family. Treating each other with such hostility simply wouldn't do. Nehemiah made sure that all the strained relationships were reconciled.

He was able to mend the tense relationships between his people by pointing them towards a common point of reference – God and His Word. Nehemiah wasn't the authority, God was. So, instead of enforcing the *Do what I say* rule, Nehemiah reminded the leaders what God had said. It was a turning back to God's statutes that brought reconciliation to the people.

You ever notice how easy it is for kids to be friends? Walk into a kindergarten class full of 5 and 6-year-olds, and everyone is friends. For the most part, they all get along with each other. Walk into a sophomore class filled with 15 and 16-year-olds, and there might be a couple of friend groups. Pockets of friend pairs. Walk into an office building filled with adults in their 30's, 40's, and 50's, and no one in the conference room may be friends. Why is that? The answer is usually found in a few things:

- Adults aren't the best at reconciling their differences
- We often don't have a common reference point to help us bridge gaps
- We carry resentments and bad memories around far too long

Relationships in training

When our kids hit their teenage years, their brains are maturing. They're transitioning from being able to only have concrete thought to gaining the capacity for more abstract thought. Reasoning becomes more developed. And because of hormone changes, emotions can be all over the place. This is why the relationships they have had since first grade may no longer appeal to them. This is also why relationships at that age can be so volatile.

It's the reason your son may "date" the same girl seven different times within the same calendar year. Something happens, so they break up. Then they get back together only to break up a week later. This is also why your daughter can be best friends with a girl one day and mortal enemies the next. Then *besties* again by the weekend. They're figuring things out. They are learning how deep a relationship can go and how meaningful a relationship can be in a person's life. They are learning how more adult relationships work.

Teenage years are a preparation for the years to come. They will need help navigating these turbulent waters. Their myriad arguments and emotional decisions may seem silly to us, but be larger than life to them. And one of the best places our kids can learn the ministry of reconciliation is in the home. From us. As godly dads, we have become Christ's ambassadors. Called into His ministry. And His ministry focused on reconciliation. He reconciled us to God and one another.

I have two daughters. For holidays like Easter and Valentine's Day, their grandparents will buy them shirts or dresses. Often the same shirts or dresses. One morning, I heard from the back of the house my two daughters screaming and threatening each other. I went to investigate to find them fighting about who gets to wear a particular dress that day because *it's just not possible for me to go to church dressed like her.* It took me a while to wrap my mind around something that seemed so ridiculous.

"You mean to tell me that both you girls have more clothes in your closets than I do, and you can't find anything to wear besides this one dress?" Both girls' eyes were beginning to moisten as they nodded their heads in agreement with my inquisition. After digging a little deeper, I discovered that the younger daughter just wanted to be like her older sister, and the older daughter wanted to be unique. After I was able to calm their emotions and explain each girl's desires and point of view to the other one, they were able to understand each other's feelings better. They made compromises that made them both happy. Ah, the sweet (and much quieter) sound of reconciliation.

Examples to follow

Our kids will learn a great deal about how relationships work and how to reconcile them through their sibling experiences. But they will also learn a lot about how relationships work from the what they observe between us and our wives. Kids are typically more perceptive than we give them credit for.

They pick up subtle comments, tone of voice, and emotions between their mom and dad.

Within reason, try to let them see how you and your wife reconcile matters. When it's appropriate, explain to them why you said or did what you did and why it was wrong. Let them hear you and your wife make things right with each other again. The next time you and your wife argue in the car on that long drive with your kids in the back overhearing every word, let them also hear the two of you apologize and say how sorry you are. Let them learn from your example.

The ultimate example of reconciliation is Jesus. He is the perfect picture of how relationships are made right. While we were still sinners and in the wrong, Christ died for us (Romans 5:8). Even though we were the ones that were wrong, Jesus was the One that took the first step towards mending the relationship. Through Christ, God no longer counted our wrongdoing against us. He taught us all to no longer view others through a worldly point of view. He gave us the ministry of reconciliation. By following His example, we know how to repair damaged relationships (2 Corinthians 5:16-21).

Teaching our kids to follow Jesus' example will not only help them be able to reconcile relationships with their friends, but also with the people they typically don't get along with. When they have a teacher they think is "just out to get me" or people at school that are "jerks to me for no reason at all," we can point to all the ways Jesus worked to have a right relationship with everyone He ever crossed paths with. We can teach them that even though we can't control how other people treat us, we can control how we treat other people. Paul said it like this, "If it is possible, as far as it depends on you, live at peace with everyone" (Romans 12:18). Our kids need to know they won't be able to fully follow God's path as long as they are living at odds with other people around them.

CONSIDER THESE QUESTIONS

- How would you describe the relationships your kids have with their friends? The people they date? Their siblings? How much of that is a reflection of your relationship with them?

- When you and your kids are at odds with each other, what do you do to reconcile the relationship? Is your approach rooted in God's Word?

- What standard of relationship does your marriage model for your kids? How could it be better?

17

BY ERIC

The Godly Dad **DEFERS** to the Needs of Others

"...neither I nor my brothers ate the food allotted to the governor."

NEHEMIAH 5:14

DURING THE SEASON, MY high school baseball team would play six games a week. Every week, we had a game on Monday, Tuesday, Thursday, Friday, and a doubleheader on Saturday. Since then, the school systems have changed the rules about how often games are allowed to be played. I can't guarantee this, but I'd guess they named the new rule after my coach.

Because of this schedule, we'd have away games at least 2-3 times a week. Regardless of how far away the game was, the team bus stopped for dinner on the way home after every game. Even if the game was only twenty minutes away, we'd stop to eat, which took at least an hour to feed the whole team. This meant I'd get home on a school night around 10 pm or later several days each week. I could never figure out why we did this. When we were so close to home, why not just drive straight back? Then it all became clear one night.

After one game that was less than ten miles away from my house, we stopped to eat. Again. I was about to place my order when our coach stepped in front of me to place his order. Because he was the coach, he didn't feel he should have to wait in the long line. After he placed his request, the cashier quoted the price of his meal. Surprised, he said, "I'm pretty sure coaches eat free." The cashier smiled, recognizing her mistake, "You're right. I'm sorry, coach." He grabbed his food and walked off.

For bringing a busload of players into their restaurant, coaches got their meal for free. In that moment, I realized our coach willingly cost us at least an extra hour on the road plus the money *we* had to pay for *our* meals several times a week so that he could get his for free. It became hard for me to see this coach in another light other than the *I come first* role he seemed to always take for himself.

Because of his work and initiation of the massive rebuild-the-wall project, Nehemiah became the governor of Jerusalem. This elevated position came with considerable perks. Certain allowances. The men who served this office before Nehemiah took advantage of these great benefits. *With great responsibility comes great power.* But not Nehemiah. He saw the position differently. He saw his position of power and authority as one used to meet the needs of those under his care. He deferred his benefits to benefit others. Do we?

Servant leadership

In the very beginning, by installing Adam as the head of the household, God established a model which put the father in the position to lead his family. Some of us take this leadership role in the wrong direction. We begin to think, like my baseball coach, *Because I'm the leader, I'm entitled to the best.* Because of this belief, we make it known throughout our family that "Dad gets the best." This could be in small ways such as dad gets the best seat in the house or the last piece of dessert. Sometimes it comes to life in much bigger ways like dad always gets the nicest car, chooses where the family vacation will be, bags the biggest Christmas presents, or doesn't have to do as many chores around the house.

Maybe as you read through those lists of items you think, *I deserve some of those perks. I've earned them.* Hmm, really? But what *should* we do with our authority? Our leadership role? To find the answer, we need only look to Jesus.

You don't need reminding of this, but Jesus was and is the Son of God. If any person deserved advantages, it was the King of kings. But when Jesus first came to earth, He wasn't royally presented in any palace or thrown a giant party with a red carpet. Instead, He spent His first night on earth wrapped up in a feeding trough in the dirt. He told those who followed Him that He didn't come to earth to be served but to serve and give His life away for others (Matthew 20:28).

He proved that His desire to meet the needs of others was greater than His desire to partake in any positional privilege. There are many instances of His taking care of the people around Him at His own expense. When Jesus was arrested in the Garden of Gethsemane, He made sure His friends were able to go free instead of freeing Himself (John 18:4-9). He spent so much time with the people who had been pushed to the margins of life that it cost Him His reputation (Matthew 9:10-11). Other than the cross itself, the best example of Jesus deferring to the needs of those around Him can be seen when He washed the disciples' feet.

As they were sharing their last meal together, Jesus stood up from the table, took the position of a servant, and began to wash the feet of His disciples. The Creator kneeling before His creation to clean their dirty feet. Interestingly, note what the Bible says about Jesus before He took on this role of foot-washer. "Jesus knew that the Father had put all things under his power...so he got up from the meal, took off his outer clothing, and wrapped a towel around his waist," (John 13:3-4). It was *because* of His authority that Jesus looked after the needs of His followers. Instead of expecting His people to make personal sacrifices due to His ultimate authority, He used His power to introduce them to servant leadership.

A massive elevation above all created things was followed immediately by a lowering of Himself to serve those around Him.

Nehemiah was a servant leader. Instead of using his role as governor to increase the comforts of his own life, Nehemiah used the benefits of his authority to help those around him. He didn't merely manage the work of the people on the walls of Jerusalem. He worked alongside them. Got dirty next to them. Gave them an example they could look to and follow. They knew how to work on the wall because they had *seen* Nehemiah doing it.

Getting rid of entitlement

Many dads gripe about *Oh, the kids today, they are so entitled!* Well, maybe – just possibly – they are acquiring this attitude of entitlement from us. It's a learned behavior. If they spend their early childhood watching us get the best of everything around the house so often that it becomes an expectation, as they approach their teenage years, they will begin to mimic our behavior. They will start to expect the best to be reserved for them. Our own selfish habits might be breeding their entitlement. Ouch, did I just type that out loud? Sorry.

If we want our kids to grow up to be generous people who consider the needs of others above their own, we must teach them this behavior through our example. It's not a lesson that just needs to be discussed. It must be modeled.

Our kids won't fully understand that we sacrifice plenty of our paychecks to meet their needs until they have kids of their own. And they won't truly understand how much personal time you gave up to drive them to practice, help coach their sporting teams, or cheer them on at their competitions. But they will be able to grasp the significance when you give them the last cookie that everyone wanted a piece of. They'll be able to discern the implications when you allow them to pick what restaurant the family eats at instead of you always having the choice.

They'll figure out what servant leadership means when you do yard work with them around the house instead of making them do it all on their own. They'll see Jesus in our actions when our actions resemble His. Or, as Paul said, "Follow my example, as I follow the example of Christ" (1 Corinthians 11:1).

The attitude of my high school coach spread throughout our team. Year after year, as underclassmen became upperclassman, they believed they'd earned certain rights. They made sure they took full advantage of them. Instead of using their experience to do what was best for the team, they claimed the best of everything for themselves. It created a toxic locker room that was only enjoyable for the seniors.

When we take on the attitude of entitlement within our families, we can create an environment that's really only fun for us. We also pass this attitude down to our kids, putting into motion a chain reaction of generations who seek after themselves. Then, we wonder where our kids get such an entitlement mentality. In humility, a godly dad will defer his privileges to his family to better meet their needs over his own.

CONSIDER THESE QUESTIONS

- Is it understood in your house that dad gets the best of things? How can you start to pull away from that mentality?

- How can you use the position of leadership in your family to better serve the members of it?

- Read through John 13:1-17. Make a note of everything Jesus did to consider the needs of His disciples over His own.

18

BY ERIC

The Godly Dad REVERES the LORD in Holy Fear

> "'...Or should someone like me go into the temple to save his life? I will not go!'"
>
> NEHEMIAH 6:11

THE WALLS WERE COMPLETE. No more gaps, minus the hanging of the gate doors that still needed to be installed. Seeing the project nearly finished, the enemy made a desperate attempt at Jerusalem's leader, Nehemiah. They tried to lure him out of the city on five different occasions, but Nehemiah sniffed out their deceptions immediately. They began with ridicule, then moved on to threats and deception. When those didn't work, the enemy tried to trick Nehemiah with a new tactic.

They hired one of Jerusalem's prophets, Shemaiah, to give Nehemiah false guidance. The prophet instructed Nehemiah, "Let us meet in the house of God, inside the temple, and let us close the temple doors, because men are coming to kill you— by night they are coming to kill you" (Nehemiah 6:10). Had he followed this poor advice Nehemiah's credibility would've been destroyed in two ways.

First, Nehemiah would've looked like a fearful leader and a hypocrite. One that encouraged boldness in his followers but who would run and hide to save his own life. Second, Nehemiah would've appeared to be a man who didn't fully follow the laws of God. By going into the temple areas reserved for priests only, Nehemiah would have been desecrating the temple. Again, Nehemiah was able to see right through this false message even as it came from the lips of a prophet. Because Nehemiah revered the LORD with holy fear, he would never do anything to intentionally contradict the Word of God.

Nehemiah was dedicated to his God. Everything he did seemed only to be done after checking in with God to make sure it lined up with His intentions. His will, not Nehemiah's. The whole book of Nehemiah is woven together by his prayers that never seem to end. Because of such devotion and commitment to God, Nehemiah was able to quickly recognize anything that was not of the Lord. This, in turn, allowed Nehemiah to lead his people unwaveringly and to avoid pitfalls along the way. His knowledge of the truth and commitment to God kept him on track, and all his people could see it in action daily.

Caught in the act

If we want our kids to grow up following Jesus, they have to see it from us. They need to see our respect for God. Our holy reverence. Our commitment to the LORD. For our kids to love God, they need to witness our love for God. They need to know that the force that drives our words, actions, and decision making is our devotion to the Creator.

For our kids to *see* our devotion to the LORD, we have to first *be* devoted to the LORD. Our focus is not staging "holy acts" for the sake of our kids to witness. The goal is to love and revere God and His Word. When our heart is genuinely devoted to our Heavenly Father, our kids will easily catch that truth from their earthly father.

David, a person known to be a man after God's own heart (1 Samuel 13:14, Acts 13:22), was committed to God. When he offered sacrifices to the LORD, they were sacrifices. They came at a cost (2 Samuel 24:24). When the ark of the covenant was moved into the city of Jerusalem, David danced in worship for the whole city to see. And he did so with all his might. Holding nothing back (2 Samuel 6:14).

Abram left everything that was familiar and everyone he knew to follow God into the unknown (Genesis 12:1-4). His willingness to set his only son on the altar as a sacrifice to

God proved that Abraham's relationship with God was the most important relationship he had (Genesis 22:1-3). The only other person there to witness Abraham's act of devotion was his son, Isaac. God honored Abraham's reverence without any grandstanding on his part. No hashtags. No postings to social media.

Jacob moved his whole family away from their homeland to follow God back to Esau and the land God was leading him towards. Before their journey, Jacob prepared his family by disposing of all their false gods (Genesis 35:2). He literally wrestled with God to find his new identity in the LORD (Genesis 32:22-28).

As Joshua stood before his people preparing them for the Promised Land, he urged them to serve God faithfully. He told the people the gods they would follow would ultimately be their choice, but his decision was already made. "But as for me and my household, we will serve the LORD."

The disciples gave up everything they had to follow after Jesus (Matthew 19:27). This commitment cost most of them their lives.

Moses stood before the king of Egypt, demanding the release of a nation of slaves (Exodus 5:1).

And the list goes on and on.

What is significant about all these amazing feats from these Biblical characters, including Nehemiah, is that they all came after significant time with the LORD or an incredible encounter with Him. Our commitment to God will begin with us spending time with Him. And this time with God will start out on our own.

Meetings with God

Quiet time. Devotional. Prayer time. Whatever you call it, there should be a time set aside for you to be alone with God. Personal time with just you and Him. For us to be devoted to God's Word, we need to know what it says. For us to understand what God is trying to tell us, we have to give Him time to speak. A time set aside for us to listen. Just like Nehemiah was able to do, when we commit ourselves to God and His Word, we will more easily recognize Him. We will also more easily identify the things that are ungodly.

Next, we must set aside time spent with God and our family. Maybe it's a family devotion that all of you have together. Maybe it's as simple as sitting around the dinner table talking about what all of you believe God is doing in your lives or what all of you are praying about or need prayers for. Whatever it is you feel led to do, there should be times when you're actively leading the way to God.

God even set up a schedule for us to make sure we instituted a time set aside for our family to focus on Him. "Remember the Sabbath day by keeping it holy" (Exodus 20:8). Don't let Sundays be jam-packed with activities and running errands. Let it be a day your family slows down to rest and talk about Jesus. If it's merely impossible to do this on Sunday, pick another day during the week as your Sabbath. It's not the particular day that is important, it's the *keeping it holy* that matters. We don't murder, carve idols out of gold, steal, nor brush those commands off as unimportant. Why would we not honor the Sabbath?

Finally, there needs to be a time focused on God with your family and other believers. "And let us consider how we may spur one another on toward love and good deeds, not giving up meeting together, as some are in the habit of doing, but encouraging one another—and all the more as you see the Day approaching" (Hebrews 10:24-25). We need to be involved in a local church, and maybe attend a Bible study or a small group. Our families need to interact with other families that are believers. They need to see how they fit in the body of Christ.

Body and spirit

Notice how the book of Nehemiah has progressed so far. The first thing Nehemiah addressed was the people of Jerusalem's physical protection. The broken-down wall full of gaps left his people vulnerable. They were open to attacks from outside enemies. This matter had to be addressed and dealt with quickly. While they were building the walls, he gave his people carpentry and mason tools for one hand and a sword for the other. Another means to protect their physical safety. After Jerusalem's physical protection had been attended to, Nehemiah turned his attention towards their spiritual condition. He focused on setting their feet back to the path that led to honoring God.

The physical protection of our family is essential. You know that. And I bet it is something you have addressed over and over. Most dads do. But, for several reasons, looking after the spiritual protection of our kids falls to the wayside more easily. Maybe it's because we can see their bodies and not their spirit that we tend to focus more on the physical. It's tangible. Measurable even. But it is not nearly as crucial as establishing their feet on the path that leads to honoring God. Nehemiah knew this truth. Before he left the people of Jerusalem, he did all he could to make sure they were dedicated to the LORD.

We can't always be with our kids. They will grow up. Move out. And move on. Before that happens, we need to do everything we can to make sure they live a life dedicated to the LORD. And the best way for that to happen is for us to live a life dedicated to revering God. It starts with us. Seeing us follow Jesus will point our kids in the same direction. "Start children off on the way they should go, and even when they are old they will not turn from it" (Proverbs 22:6).

CONSIDER THESE QUESTIONS

- If your kids were asked, what would they say is the most important thing in your life? Why would they list that as their answer?

- What does your personal time with God look like? How is that working for you? What does your family's time with God look like? How is that working for them?

- In your mind, picture a man that reveres God. What characteristics does that guy have? How does he spend his time? His money? Pick one or two of these answers to start implementing this week.

19

BY ERIC

The Godly Dad **ANTICIPATES** That Trouble Will Arise

"I realized that God had not sent him..."

NEHEMIAH 6:12

WHEN I WAS IN fifth grade, computer-generated images called Magic Eye came out and instantly became popular. These were pictures that looked like random ink dots with 3D images hidden within them. I still remember the first time I ever saw one. It was a page filled with countless squiggly orange lines with the word "Dinosaurs" written underneath it. I had no idea what I was looking at, but one thing I knew for sure: there weren't any dinosaurs in that picture. I stared at it for about ten minutes, searching for any sign of dinosaurs. A claw, some teeth. Nothing. Then, this kid who looked to be three or four years younger than me walked up beside me to take a peek. After maybe eight seconds, he blurted out, "Aw, man! That's an awesome T-Rex!" Then he walked off. I wanted to punch him.

After 15 minutes of glaring into the void of this digital oblivion, my eyes started to hurt, so I left. Not a single dinosaur seen. And I was also pretty sure the kid who claimed to see a T-Rex was a liar. Within a couple of weeks, a friend of mine from school brought a book to class filled with Magic Eye pictures. Because he could see all the hidden images, he told me what I needed to do to be able to see them too. Once I learned how, I was able to see things clearly and instantly. I could recognize what lay beneath the surface every time I looked at one of those pictures. Then, I was the one who'd walk up to other people and show-off my amazing powers of depth perception.

Because Nehemiah was chasing a godly objective, he faced opposition. Unfriendly characters were trying to create trouble for him. These enemies intended real, physical harm to Nehemiah. This wasn't metaphorical.

Once the wall was all but finished, these foes sent a message to Nehemiah for a meeting. It was set for a nearby village in the plain of Ono. This area was about 27 miles northwest of Jerusalem. Just outside of Jewish territory and near the hostile regions of Samaria and Ashdod. Nehemiah instantly sniffed out the danger. Just like I learned to do with the Magic Eye images, Nehemiah could see past the surface of their invitation. Their message of *Hey, Nehemiah. We should meet near some of my friends that hate you as much as we do and just talk a bit,* didn't fool Nehemiah for a second. He could anticipate the trouble that lay ahead with these people.

I wonder if Nehemiah had people in Jerusalem who could make Magic Eye sand drawings. Hmm? Anyway, let's move on.

Looking ahead

As a dad trying to raise our kids in a godly home, we need to know that troubles will arise. There will be opposition. Dangers around the corner. We must learn to anticipate them. Be ready.

Kent has a friend he once overheard pray, "God, please help me and my wife see trouble when it is still far off." A wise move. This guy was asking the One who sees all to help him understand potential threats while they are still far enough away to potentially head them off. He was seeking other-worldly insights. We need to not only be able to recognize trouble when we see it. We also need to be able to identify the situations and people that could *lead* to trouble. Even just the possibility of danger. This ability will come from God. He can signal our hearts and spirits to be alert for coming problems many times before they are on our doorstep. He did it for Nehemiah.

Nehemiah went to see a prophet named Shemaiah. When he suggested an unusual meeting place for the two of them to continue their conversation – the temple – Nehemiah knew something wasn't right. Depending on which translation you use, the Bible tells us that Nehemiah *realized* or *understood* or *perceived* that God was not in the advice of Shemaiah. This immediate discernment on Nehemiah's part came from God. Nehemiah could anticipate trouble before it became trouble because he listened to God's whispering.

After my college soccer team would play a game, we would all meet in the field house to review a replay of the match on video. Many times, as I watched myself, I would wonder *What was I thinking there? How could I not see that coming?* Sometimes I didn't even have to think it. It was audibly pointed out to me from my coach, "*Ballard, what were you thinking? How could you not see that coming? You gotta learn to pick up on that stuff before it happens. Anticipate.*" He said that word "anticipate" so often, it still echoes in my mind. I used to anticipate him screaming "Anticipate!"

It's always easier to see trouble and mistakes in hindsight. As godly dads, we have to learn to anticipate as many as we possibly can. See them coming. Recognize the danger before it gets so close to us it's too late to avoid. Just like Nehemiah did.

Trouble comes from everywhere

It's also important to know that trouble doesn't always come at us from dubious places in the far-off distance. Sometimes problems come from within. The messages sent from Nehemiah's enemies came from outside the walls. Outsiders. But the prophet Shemaiah was an insider. He lied to Nehemiah in an effort to frighten him into teaming up with his enemies. This one came from within the walls. One of Nehemiah's own people. We have to learn to anticipate the trouble that comes from without and the kind of trouble that comes from within. Even within our own families.

I'm going to let you in on one of the worst kept secrets of all time. Kids mess up. There, I said it. They make mistakes. They find their way into trouble. Even your precious little angel who's never done one wrong thing in his life. He too, can be (eh-hem, will be) a troublemaker. We have to anticipate and expect our kids to act like kids.

If we know what to expect, we won't wind up as frustrated when it happens. We must align our expectations with reality. This will help us see trouble before it hits us and knocks us off balance. And when it comes to our kids, the truth is, they're going to tell lies now and then. They're going to cheat. Act selfishly. Be a little forgetful. Put simply, at times, they are going to say things they shouldn't say and do things they shouldn't do. The reason they do these things is because they are sinful. Just like you and me. Sinners sin. It happens.

Will our kids make poor choices? That's not the question we need to focus on. They absolutely will. The real question we need to consider is *how do we prevent our kids from making the kind of poor choices that have major, life-altering* consequences? *How do we protect them from the dangers they are unable to see?* The answer is anticipation. And, in some cases, despite our best efforts and God-given discernment, they will still get off track. Way off track. We can't prevent every danger or bad choice. That's above our pay grade.

Discernment leads to anticipation

Nehemiah had this knack for seeing *potential* trouble, so he was able to avoid it before any real damage was done. This ability didn't come from himself. Nehemiah was a man of prayer. And this lifestyle habit of constant communication with God gave him wisdom and discernment to see around the corner. The more time we spend with God, the more easily we will recognize Him at work. But we will also gain the ability to identify the ungodly. That's discernment, and it's a crucial element in developing the skill of godly anticipation.

During my sophomore year of college, I went over to a buddy's dorm room. The room was full of people. Most of the guys there, I knew. Some I didn't. I had walked into that room dozens of times before, but, for some reason, this time felt different. Something wasn't right. I couldn't quite put my finger on what it was, but something was just…off. I didn't see or hear anything that set off mental alarms. Somehow, I just knew, *I'm not supposed to be here.* So, I left. Later that night, a couple of the guys in that room got arrested for poor choices. They even called me to come bail them out around two in the morning. If I had been with them, I could have lost my athletic scholarship, which would have put me in a world of trouble. I was grateful that God's Holy Spirit guided me that night. And, that I listened.

Learning to recognize that *something's just not right here* feeling the Holy Spirit nudges us with is the key to anticipating the trouble that lies ahead. It is an insight from God that should not go ignored. The quicker we act on God's guidance, the better off we will be. We just have to recognize how God speaks to us.

Maybe, for reasons you can't fully explain, your finances are always on your mind. Having enough money has never really been a worry before, but now, it's all you think about. It might be time to anticipate financial trouble. Start addressing possible problems like debt piling up, living outside your means, or your "rainy day" fund that you've allowed to dwindle.

Is there a guy at work who keeps living right on the edge of some shady practices? His results aren't lining up with his work. Anticipate the next problem. You know how true this is: people who do dishonest work with others will eventually be the same people playing dirty with you too.

Maybe there's been some real tension between you and your wife over the last couple of weeks. In anticipation of marital conflict, you should start praying for your wife. Sit down with her and have that tough conversation. Figure out what's going on between the two of you before any painful damage is done.

Trying to live and lead as a godly dad ensures you will face adversaries. Trouble. Lean on God to point out those dangers while they are still off in the distance. Pray for God to give you discernment so you can anticipate trouble before it becomes a crisis. Then, have the courage to buckle down and make the right choices to avoid as much of it as you possibly can.

CONSIDER THESE QUESTIONS

- How was Nehemiah able to consistently anticipate threats of trouble? How could his strategy work for you?

- How can spending more time with God help you recognize His voice more clearly?

- What unseen trouble do you think you should be anticipating right now? Why do you feel that way? What are you going to do about this anticipation?

20

The Godly Dad **RELIES** Only on God's Strength

"...they realized that this work had been done with the help of our God."

NEHEMIAH 6:16

WHEN I WAS ABOUT seven years old, my dad brought home a puppy for my sister and me. A small brown and white boxer. We named him Tobo. The first few weeks we had Tobo, I took him everywhere. I'd pick him up and put him in my bed when it was time to sleep. I'm pretty sure I even tried to put him into the bath with me.

As Tobo got a little older, we'd wrestle around in our living room. Because he was an animal, there were times during our wrestling matches where he would get a little too worked up and fight a little too hard. Started to try and bite me. Whenever he would do this, I'd just pick him up off the ground to take away his leverage. I would then hold him in the air until he calmed down. Before Tobo was even a year old, something changed. He had gotten a lot bigger in the months we had him, while I stayed pretty much the same size. He was too big for me to pick up. I could no longer control him like I once could. It had gotten to the point when we wrestled that he had the advantage. But because of all the time we spent tussling when he was smaller, he knew when he started to hurt me for real and would stop on his own.

Jerusalem's walls were rebuilt. No more gaps. No more points of vulnerability. The incredibly large construction project Nehemiah had championed was complete. The stones in that wall were probably put into place with plenty of blood and sweat from the people of Jerusalem. Maybe even some tears. A true feat of strength and determination they could be proud of. But it wasn't only their strength that raised those walls. There was a much bigger Strength at work. Nehemiah trusted more in God's power to rebuild Jerusalem's walls than he did his own (2:20). That's what made the project so successful.

A strength beyond our own

You may be an incredibly talented man. Strong. Wise. With an endless list of skills and abilities. Almost as good looking as me. Even with all those talents, if you think you can be a godly father on your own strength, you are fooling yourself. Chances are you've tried. You've used all the capabilities you have at your disposal and realized; *I can't do this. Not very well, anyway. I'm not the dad I could be.* If that realization hasn't hit you yet, it's probably because your kids are still young. Give it time. It's coming.

I have a daughter in the fourth grade. There have been times she has come home from school to tell me about a day that didn't go her way. As she details how her feelings were hurt, my first thought is almost always, *I don't have the right words to say here.* I want to help. To make everything okay. To go beat up whatever kids made her feel bad. Their dads too. But I can't help in the way she needs it. I can't take the pain away. It's beyond my control. This cycle of events is only going to get worse as she gets older. As our kids grow, just like my dog Tobo did, their issues and problems will get too big for us to pick up and manhandle. While our personal strength can only take us so far, there is One who has the power to overcome all circumstances. Nehemiah relied on God's strength, and so should we.

While the rebuild project of the wall was still in its early phases, Nehemiah's efforts were mocked ruthlessly. One of the naysayers described the walls as so brittle that even if a fox hopped along the top, it would be enough to break down the stone structure (4:3). Instead of personally going after his enemies, Nehemiah turned to God's strength. He asked God to, "Turn their insults back on their own heads. Give them over as plunder in a land of captivity" (4:4). That's the prayer of a man who trusted in God to take action with a strength he didn't possess himself.

Unexplainable strength

God's strength works in ways we can't fully understand. Most of the time, we can only shake our heads and say, *Well, that must have been God.* In possibly one of the most famous stories in the entire Bible, a young boy named David took on a literal giant warrior named Goliath. David took down the titan without a single injury to himself. Not even a scrape. David made it clear to the giant, and everyone else gathered that day, he wasn't coming out to fight in his own strength. He was coming to battle in the strength and name of the LORD (1 Samuel 17:45). That fight lasted all of 10 seconds. I'm sure all the Israelites cowering behind David saw Goliath fall and shook their heads while they said to one another, *Well, that must have been God.*

Because His strength can allow us to do things we couldn't do on our own, we must go to God and rely entirely on His strength. One of the strongest things you can do as a godly father is to ask God to give you strength. Then rely on His strength above your own.

160 | ERIC BALLARD

Here are just a few types of strength we will need to help us push ever forward as a godly father.

Patience. As we've discussed in previous chapters, our kids are going to make mistakes. Probably a lot of them. On some occasions, we are going to need supernatural patience to deal with them. Godly patience that will help us remain calm and prevents us from making things worse by blowing up and saying or doing hurtful things we can't take back. Patience is an act of love where we bear one another's shortcomings (Ephesians 4:2).

The right words to say. There is a saying out there that states *Truth is stranger than fiction*. Some of the situations our kids will find themselves in will boggle the mind. You will have no words. Not the right ones, anyway. We need God to give us the words to help our kids. Strong words. The kind that can speak healing into a broken heart. Words that can assure them everything is going to be okay. The right words at the right moment can breathe life back into kids who are ready to give up. Godly fathers should ask their Heavenly Father to fill their mouths with His words (Jeremiah 1:9).

Humility needed to apologize. Our kids are going to make mistakes. But so are we. There are going to be times and circumstances that we get wrong. Situations we mishandle. We blow it. It will take strength to admit our mistakes and ask for our kids' forgiveness. It's a difficult process, but one that teaches our kids a life lesson they won't soon forget. They'll see we're human. They'll know that no one is above taking ownership and responsibility for their misdoings. They'll see our love for them is strong because humility takes strength.

Obviously strong

When the source of our strength comes from the LORD, instead of ourselves, people will take notice. When the wall of Jerusalem was finished, Nehemiah didn't have to tell people the project was finished with the help of God's strength. They knew it. It was obvious.

At the dedication of the wall, the people of Jerusalem rejoiced greatly in the work God had done through them. Their celebration was so grand, echoes of it could be heard from far away (12:43). Their rejoicing was great. And because of Nehemiah, they knew their joy in the LORD was the source of their strength (8:10).

Exercising God's strength will make it apparent to those around us, and even far off, that we are working with a power that is beyond our capability. They'll take notice. This includes our kids. Our conversations about Jesus will be impactful. But when they see us living out a strength that comes from God, it will leave an impression that words never could. It can be the kind of significant influence that sticks with them long after they grow past the ages where we no longer have control over them.

While our control over our kids diminishes as they grow older, our influence can carry on forever. In fact, I'd argue that our influence with our children should grow as they mature. It should carry on even beyond our grave, in a sense.

For us to have a lasting impact on our kids, we will have to operate on a system that relies on God's strength. We are only human. A sin-stained history that we inherited from our forefathers has made us weak. We have limitations. A lot of them. To demonstrate an everlasting strength for our kids, we must point them towards the Everlasting One! We can't handle all of our family's problems on our own strength. Won't happen. Simply not possible. So, don't try. Turn to God instead. When we find joy in who He is, we will also find a limitless strength.

CONSIDER THESE QUESTIONS

- When it comes to leading your family, what areas do you feel secure in? What aspects do you think you need more strength in?

- How have you demonstrated God's strength in your life for your family? Do they think of you as strong or God as strong? Is it okay for them to think of both as strong? Why or why not?

- What is one or two lasting truths or character traits you hope your kids carry with them once you are no longer around? What are you doing to ensure they know that truth or character trait?

21

BY KENT

The Godly Dad **REFLECTS** on the Past and Learns from It

> "...I found the genealogical record of those who had been the first to return..."
>
> *NEHEMIAH 7:5*

I ONCE WORKED FOR a large corporation. They had billions in sales and hundreds of offices around the world. I landed on a project sponsored by the Chief Marketing Officer of the whole company. It was a high-profile endeavor. Unfortunately, midway through the project, that CMO left the company and a new one was brought in.

Soon after the new guy arrived, he and I met together at a corporate event in Berlin, Germany. He was a brash, aggressive and outspoken man. If you're kind, you'd call his approach "confident." If you were ditching euphemisms, words like arrogant and pushy might be a bit more on target.

I was giving him a brief history on this project – how it began, who they key players were and how it was organized. Just giving him a lay of the land, so we could get on with how he wanted to shape it going forward. I also wanted to give him a heads up on what his boss (yep, that'd be the CEO) thought of the project.

About five minutes in, he interrupted with a raised hand toward my face, "You know, Kent, I don't really care about the past or how we got here. I'm noticing that a lotta things around here weren't done the way I'd like. So, whatever approach has been taken probably needs some changing."

Now, on one hand, I appreciated his perspective. Focusing on the past was probably a bad idea, and there were ways we could improve for sure. But on the other hand, this was a million-dollar project with support at every level of the company. Deciding to shift it was certainly his call. But, just labeling it a wayward and unproductive effort? Well, that was probably not going to land well on the desks of some of his powerful colleagues who'd endorsed it.

There's a difference between *focusing on* the past and *learning from* it. In his case, he did neither. In his effort to avoid the former, he didn't do the latter either.

Sure enough, in less than one year, he was booted, and a new CMO was hired. It's one thing to be the "new sheriff in town" and start enforcing laws as they should've been all along. It's another to come in guns blazing just shooting at anything that moves, especially those things that weren't your idea.

What we see in Nehemiah's approach is a perfect blend of learning from the past while still charting the future. In later chapters, we'll take a closer look at how Nehemiah righted some wrongs and reestablished some customs to get these wayward Israelites back on track. But, at the same time, he also looked intently at the past and mined valuable lessons from it.

Honoring those who've gone before

In chapter 7, Nehemiah starts to put together a census. As he does, he finds the book of genealogy which listed those who came up first from the exile. These were people who'd been in Babylon for 70 years, and they were some of the first to return to Jerusalem. As commentator David Guzik says it, these were people who had the "pioneer spirit – and they are mentioned *twice* in God's eternal word (here and Ezra 2)." Some of Israel's greatest generation.

By doing this, Nehemiah was accomplishing a few things. First, he was capturing names for organizational purposes. They had to make decisions about who'd live where, and this list was a great starting point. Second, he was honoring those who took the risk and returned by listing their names in his annals. Third, he was establishing a pattern for future leaders. When you take over, know your people well and reflect on what's occurred before you.

It's tempting as fathers to bust in with our approach and take over. We see our kids trying to open a jar, and we snag it out of their hand, "Lemme show you how it's done!" We see our wife struggling with a lost friendship, and we want to tell her, "Just get over it, and move on." Or we hear a phone conversation our daughter has with a classmate, and as soon as she gets off the phone, we're starting in with our thoughts on what she said and how she said it.

We sometimes have a surplus of opinion combined with a deficiency of context. We must be careful here. We usually would benefit from more context and perspective, not less. This is extremely true in our marriages and families.

Always in a hurry

Have you ever learned something about your past that unlocked a new understanding for you? My wife and kids will tell you that I'm usually in a hurry. I talk fast. I move fast. I want to get in the car fast. After dinner, I want it cleaned up fast. I pray regularly asking God to help me be more patient. Why am I like this?

Well, partly, because God's not done with me yet. His Spirit is still smoothing out my rough edges, and patience is a particularly rough one. But also, this was a pattern I learned from my own dad. In many ways, he was a solid dad. I'm not

168 | KENT EVANS

chalking up who I am at fifty years to how I was raised. God redeems and restores. I'm not a victim of my upbringing.

Even so, if you know my dad, you'd agree that patience wasn't (and isn't) one of his strongest character traits. Whether he's playing golf and unhappy with the pace of the group in front of us, or he's driving somewhere and can't get "all these yo-yo's" off the road in front of him, he is usually in a hurry. He's in his eighties now and still has that forward tilt!

As fathers, we do well to do some digging in our own pasts to learn how we got to where we are. And, we should do this in the pasts of our family members as well.

Looking through their lens

Maybe you're a stepdad leading a blended family. Your children have a past, and while you might want to help them find a better future, you do need to be aware of the events and people who shaped them and how they think.

Even if you've raised children since birth, reflecting on the road they've walked can help you understand how they're thinking or feeling. You mentally drop into their world and try to think about how you'd process their lives in first person.

What did your son learn from that time he missed (or made) the game-winning shot? What did it do to your daughter when that boy broke her heart (or told her he loved her)? What is it like to live with a dad like you, who has a pattern of being critical (or of being encouraging)? Can you envision the road they've walked?

What was it like for your wife growing up? How did her siblings treat her? Did she have an encouraging, loving, earthly dad? Or one who abandoned her when she was young? Our experiences shape our perceptions.

My wife is an amazing cook. Preparing food is in her DNA. Like Elton John's pinball wizard, she *becomes part of the machine, feeling all the frying pans, always cooking clean. She cooks by intuition, and I've never seen her fall.* Well, except that one time.

She decided to fix a meal featured on a cooking show. It was called "Drunken Chicken," and it called for wine. But, we don't drink wine. Nevertheless, I hopped up to the nearby Party Mart and bought a random bottle of wine (read: one I could afford).

A first-time recipe with a key ingredient picked out by an uneducated buyer (me)? That spelled disaster. It was horrible, as in, not edible. It's been years, but, if you called our older kids right now and asked them about an awful dinner we've had, they'd instantly reply, "Drunken Chicken." Never again. My wife has fixed us at least 20,000 meals and is the only one we'd never ask her to make again. Ever.

So, is "Drunken Chicken" a bad meal? Well, *to us* it is. Our past affects our present. Said another way, our past affects how *we view* our present. You may give the same set of experiences to two different people, but how they interpret them is filtered. They're viewed through their beliefs, opinions and paradigms. Those perception tools were shaped by what they did, read, said and heard before. Their past.

For dads, this idea of "filtering" is crucial for us to understand, both for ourselves and our family members. If our wives were abandoned by their dad, then, any time we are unaccountable, it can trigger those same feelings of fear and loss. If our children have been told by teachers or classmates that they're stupid, then, any form of feedback might cause them to become defensive and angry. Our experiences have a powerful influence over our world view.

Who you learn from

I once heard a powerful speaker say, "Two things will shape who you'll be in five years. The people you hang out with and what you read." There's a lot of truth in that. If our next five years shape who we'll become, then what have our last five years been doing?

This idea of hanging out with good people and reading quality material extends beyond those alive in this era. We can learn from a past way beyond the decades we've been walking on this earth. Our learning timetable can stretch back into history so we can gain valuable experience from those who've gone before us.

You'll see in Nehemiah that he references many events that occurred and people who lived long before his time. He heard the ancient stories. He read the history of Israel. He knew about the heroes of old. From that deep well of history he could draw up ideas, lessons and strategies that informed his leadership.

You and I must do the same.

CONSIDER THESE QUESTIONS

- Who are some Biblical heroes you identify with? How well do you know their stories? Why not dive in and learn more about them?

- What are some major events in your life that shaped your views and beliefs? Did they make your paradigm more or less aligned to the truth of scripture?

- When was a time that you didn't have sufficient context and you made a bad decision? How could a respect for the past have helped you avoid the pitfall?

22

BY ERIC

The Godly Dad **PROCLAIMS** God's Word Regularly

"They told Ezra the teacher of the Law to bring out the Book of the Law of Moses."

NEHEMIAH 8:1

I LOVE SPORTS. ALL sports. I played as much and as many of them as I could growing up. Four in high school and one in college. Of all the sports I played, at some point or another, my dad was my coach in most of them. Because of this, we got to spend a lot of time together. Practice. Weekend tournaments. Road trips to the games. Even when we weren't on the field or court, we would spend a lot of time at home around the dinner table discussing games and practice of whatever sport was in season at the time.

But what my dad and I seldom talked about was the Bible. It rarely came up. I'm assuming because my dad had a lengthy sports background himself, he felt capable and qualified to coach me in almost any sport I wanted to play. And because his knowledge of Scripture was less extensive, his coaching on the Bible was also less extensive.

My story is not an uncommon one. Sports fields across the world are filled with dads taking on the role of coach and trainer, teaching their kids the finer skills of athletic games. But if you walk into a majority of churches in America, the volunteer roles of small group leaders and Sunday school teachers aren't typically filled by dads.

Part of the issue with the lack of involvement from dads at church is the fact that we tend to compartmentalize all the responsibilities of raising our kids. School teachers will take care of all their educational needs. Doctors will care for all their illnesses. Personal trainers will help them get stronger or work on their homerun swing. And pastors will teach them the Bible. That's their jobs, right? Yes and no.

All those professions are available to help our kids. But they are also, for the most part, supplementary to our leading. Doctors don't come to your house to make sure your kids are following a healthy diet, to clean all the cut elbows and scraped up knees, or protect them from physical harm. Doctors are there for emergencies. Dentists don't come over in the morning or around bedtime to teach your kids how to brush their teeth. That's our job.

It's our responsibility to care for the rest of their physical well-being. And in the scope of eternity, spiritual health is far more vital than all other aspects of our kids' growth.

Nehemiah had become the governor of Jerusalem, and that role, which he took very seriously, put a lot of people under Nehemiah's care and leadership. He saw one of his chief priorities to be proclaiming God's word to his people regularly. Before Nehemiah showed up, the people of Jerusalem had fallen away from God. They had forgotten about God's Law. *Not on Nehemiah's watch.*

He brought all the people out into the town square and, knowing that not everyone would know how to read, had God's Word read to them out loud. Nehemiah knew for his people to be changed and grow closer to God, they would have to hear and understand God's words. And he was right. Hearing God's Law for the first time or for the first time in a long time, the people were affected deeply and wept as the words of God washed over them. Nehemiah led his people into knowing God's words, and so should we.

Just in case you are unaware of this truth, you are a pastor. As a follower of Jesus, you have become a priest. "But you are a chosen people, a royal priesthood, a holy nation, God's special possession, that you may declare the praises of him who called you out of darkness into his wonderful light" (1 Peter 2:9). With that in mind, dear reverend, your flock lives under your roof. You are the pastor in your home. And as Peter said in his letter, you are to declare the praises of the One that delivered you out of the darkness. Just like Nehemiah, you must proclaim God's words regularly.

To pass on God's Word and all the life-giving scripture found inside, you have to know God's Word. You can't teach what you don't know. Here are a few steps to help you get more comfortable with the Bible so that you will be able to talk about it more easily. You may want to try and tackle all of them at the same time, but I wouldn't recommend it. Your first training session preparing for a triathlon wouldn't include *completing* a triathlon. You'd start smaller by picking one skill to practice first. Read through the list below and pray about choosing *one* to master over the next 30 days. At the end of 30 days, pick another skill to add to your arsenal.

Create a time and space

One of the best ways for your kids to see the importance of God's Word in their lives is to see it in ours. If you are reading this book, and there's not really any pictures so you gotta be reading it, you probably believe the Bible is essential. But do your actions match your beliefs? Do you spend time alone in God's Word? I know, I know. You're busy. If you had more time, you'd spend more time studying the Bible, right? But you have a job, family, kids, *stuff is going on.*

The truth is, we men make time for what's important to us. Spend a couple of hours watching the game this week? Find a way to squeeze in nine holes? Climb a deer stand lately? Gone fishing? Do any work around the garage? If it matters enough, we can make the time.

Ten minutes. Give ten dedicated minutes every day to God. Read for five minutes, then pray about what you read for five minutes. When you do it or how much you read doesn't matter in the beginning. The Bible is a living, active book (Hebrews 4:12). Spending time in it regularly will change you. The more times you open the Bible, the more opportunities you give God to draw you into His Word.

Bring a notebook

When I was in high school, I asked my youth pastor (the guy I thought knew the Bible better than anyone I had ever met), "How do you study your Bible?" He gave me several practical tips, one of which was to keep a journal. Now, he said *journal*, but I heard *diary*. There's no way I'm doing that, I thought. *I'm no sissy* (I was a really manly high schooler). But because I respected my youth pastor so much, I tried his advice.

When I would read through a passage of scripture, I would write down my thoughts, questions I had, what I thought God might be saying to me through His words, and anything that stood out to me. It was difficult at first but quickly became a vital discipline that I still practice today. By keeping all those old notebooks, I can go back and look at how God has spoken to me in my past compared to how He speaks to me now. Having a record of all the ways God has spoken to you is a powerful archive to possess.

Commit it to memory

There is something about memorizing scripture. It becomes part of you. During the times in my life where I have focused on scripture memory, God's Word has always been there for me, even without me trying to recall it. When faced with tough decisions or situations, verses I'd memorized would just pop in my head. It was God's way of speaking to me through His Word without His Word being physically present. Memorized scripture is like carrying around a loaded weapon on a duck hunt; whatever flies out of the sky, you're ready. Start committing one verse to memory a week.

Share what you know

Talking about God's Word keeps it a constant in your life. You don't have to know everything about the Bible before you starting trying to share it with your kids. You don't have to be an expert. You don't know as much about football as Bill Belichick, but you've probably tried to show your kids how to throw a spiral. Teach what you know. When they have questions you don't understand, research it together or ask someone else. Plus, it's okay to answer a question about God with, *I don't know.* If you could know all there is to know about God, He wouldn't really be God, would He?

The most important thing you can pass down to your kids is a love for God and His Word. To do that, you need to proclaim it regularly. And to proclaim it, you got to know it.

So, spend time in God's Word. It will change your life and the life of your kids.

CONSIDER THESE QUESTIONS

- What would it take for you to feel more comfortable talking about God and His Word with anyone and everyone? Are you actively taking steps to get there?

- What is one step you are going to take to have a better understanding of God's Word for the next 30 days?

- Add some accountability. Tell a buddy about the efforts you are taking to get to know God better. Tell him to periodically ask you about it over the next couple of weeks. Ask him to join you on your journey.

23

BY ERIC

The Godly Dad **PROMISES** to Keep God's Commands

> " '...we are making a binding agreement, putting it in writing, and our leaders...are affixing their seals to it.' "
>
> *NEHEMIAH 9:38*

I DON'T ENJOY CONFRONTATION. I'll do it when it's called for, but it's not something I eagerly look forward to doing. While it makes me a little uncomfortable now, I used to hate it. For a couple of summers in college, I was a lifeguard at the YMCA. Great job. Loved it. I got to spend the whole summer sitting around the poolside while getting paid to do it. The only downside was the occasional confrontation with people that thought the rules didn't apply to them. *I know we're not supposed to have any food on the pool deck, but I'm special.* No, you're not.

My first summer as a lifeguard was the first summer this particular YMCA was open. Because everything was new, occasionally, people would genuinely break the rules out of ignorance. They didn't know they couldn't bring their inflatable pool toys from home or blast their 90's grunge music at full blast. After a couple of weeks of lifeguards constantly repeating the same corrections over and over again, the YMCA posted a massive sign on the wall next to the pool with all the rules spelled out. Once it was written down for everyone to see, people knew what the expectations were and did what they were supposed to. Made my job a lot easier.

After God's Law was read aloud to all the people of Jerusalem, their eyes were opened to the truth. And it broke them. They wept at the thought of how far they had strayed from God. They wanted to make things right again. They wanted to return to their First Love. So, they confessed their sins. They made promises and commitments to keeping God's commands. In an attempt to take things up a notch, they converted their commitments into a binding agreement.

Which direction to go

As a godly father, we are the ones called to lead our family. But where are we leading them? *Closer to God.* Good answer, but a little on the vague side. How are you leading them closer to God? Are there benchmarks you're moving towards? Are there any goals you are pushing your family to reach? Is there a specific mission you want to achieve with your family? What is the vision God has placed on your heart for your family?

That last paragraph is a tough one. Some hard questions that most of us will answer with *I don't know.* That's okay. We have to start somewhere. And like almost anything that truly matters in this life, the first thing we need to do to find answers is pray. We have to talk to God to find the direction He wants us to go.

When God first met with Abraham, He called the patriarch to leave everything he knew behind to go...where, exactly? Abraham didn't know. Abraham wasn't told. The only direction God gave Abraham was that he was to go, "to the land I will show you" (Genesis 12:1). Abraham knew he was supposed to leave, but he wasn't told where to go. The only way Abraham would know what the *next* step in his journey would be was by taking the *first* step. His departure from his homeland was a visual promise to every one of his obedience to God's calling. When you are planning out the roadmap of your family's spiritual journey, you may only know the first step. The destination may be unclear, but you know where the first stop is. That's good enough. Like Abraham, move towards that first step and trust God to reveal the next one when you get there.

Paul was one of the first Christian missionaries. He was the one trusted with the mission of carrying the gospel to the Gentiles (Acts 22:21). Knowing this, Paul told the other apostles he would minister to the Gentiles (Galatians 2:9). And in the beginning, that's really all Paul knew for sure. He knew he was called to share Jesus with people outside of the Jewish traditions. He couldn't know what would happen when he arrived in each new town. He was never absolutely sure how things would go down. But he went, just as he had "promised" the other apostles he would, and God showed Paul how to approach each new Gentile region.

Once you know the direction God wants you to go, go. Then, like Abraham and Paul, tell others about it. Make it real. Make it a promise. Let those close to you hold you accountable to that promise. Then, also like Abraham and Paul, keep going back to God for guidance. It will be a process we have to go through continually. Over and over again, we will need directions. It's better to seek God's guidance than our instincts.

Keep going

In the Old Testament, the prophet Elijah was an impressive dude. When all the other prophets of God were gone or in hiding, Elijah went right after King Ahab, Queen Jezebel, and their 850 false prophets. He arranged a showdown on Mount Carmel between him and these 850 prophets or, more accurately, the One True God versus Baal.

In this epic clash, God showed up in a significant way and proved in front of everyone that He is, in fact, God. Consequently, all the prophets of Baal were executed. It was quite the victory for God and Elijah, who carried the banner of God alone. Instead of celebrating, Elijah ran away. Alone and afraid, Elijah wanted to give up. After such a huge God moment, Elijah wanted to quit. He had lost his way somehow and didn't want to go on any further. Instead, an angel of the Lord gave Elijah provisions and instruction. This gave him the strength to move towards having another encounter with God. And from there, God directed Elijah to meet with Elisha. And the cycle repeated (1 Kings 18-19).

While you are leading your family into the mystery where God can be found, you may lose your way at times. Don't quit. Don't give up. Pray for the provisions you need to move to your next meeting place with God. He'll give you what you need. And once you make it to that destination, He'll provide you with direction to the next meeting place.

Again, you don't need to have the entire spiritual route identified. You just need to know where the next stop should be and the strength to get there. Once you know that much, tell your family. It's not a secret. Nor a need-to-know basis. Share God's plan and leading with your family. Let them in on the mission and make it clear what you all will be doing to get there. Nehemiah felt it best to write these things down in a binding agreement. Nehemiah made sure his promises were of the visible sort.

Promise keeper

Try this quick exercise. Make a quick list of people in your family. Beside each name, write down any significant promises you've made to or for that person. Wedding vows to your wife. Promises to teach and train up your kids in the LORD. Promises of protection. How are you doing on fulfilling those promises? Do any of them need refreshing? Any new promises need to be added to the list? Have you broken any of them? Keep this list as a reminder. Better yet, show it to the people you have made the promises. Remind them of your intentions.

Making our promises known to our family will help us stay on task. Keep us accountable to our promises. And having them written down will make it easier for the whole family to have visible reminders of what those promises are. This can be done in any number of ways. Maybe all of you sit down together and come up with a family mission statement. Every year around the same time, you guys revisit and make amendments to the mission statement. As the family grows, so should the promises. Maybe you come up with several reminder cards of scripture verses that are important to your family, then you place them around the house in prominent places. Anytime one of you sees a card, you are reminded of the promises you have made. Like seeing the pool rules written on the wall at the YMCA, people will know what's expected.

There is something about resolutions and confession and promises being put in writing. Nehemiah did it as a reminder for all his people to keep the promises that were made. Give his example a try. Ask God to show you where He wants you to lead your family. Then make those plans known to your family. Seal it with a written promise.

CONSIDER THESE QUESTIONS

- What's one thing you know God has called you to lead your family towards? Write it down on an index card and post it on your refrigerator.

- How can you include your whole family in the process of making promises to God?

- Who is a trusted friend of yours that is also a godly dad? Tell him about the promises you have made with and for your family. Next month, tell him the progress you've made on that promise.

24

BY ERIC

The Godly Dad **TITHES** from His First Fruits

"...each of our families is to bring...a contribution to burn on the altar...as it is written in the Law."

NEHEMIAH 10:34

I WAS IN COLLEGE when this story took place. You must keep that in mind as you read through it.

While I am not an intelligent adult, I was an even dumber kid. With that disclaimer, I was dating a girl that had recently graduated and was starting her career as a teacher. We had only been dating for a couple of weeks when I joined her and her family at their church. When the offering plate came around, my date dropped in a dollar. I saw that and started a bad train of thought. I knew teachers didn't make a lot of money, but I knew they had to make more than ten bucks a week. I became super judgmental and felt I needed to say something (Again, remember the disclaimer—really dumb kid).

On the car ride to lunch, I tried to think of a tactful way to bring up the "offering incident." Despite my lack of wisdom, even I knew I couldn't simply blurt out, *What's the deal with only giving God a dollar, you sinner.* As I searched for the right words, she brought the topic up for me. "Did you see my aunt?" she questioned, "she put $100 in the offering plate." I did the quick math and said, "That's probably about right, I would think." She shook her head in disbelief, "I don't think I could ever give that much money to the church."

If I'm completely honest, which I guess I should be, after that I knew we wouldn't date long. And we didn't. It wasn't the amount of money she gave that bothered me. It was the heart it reflected. Again, I was being super judgmental and made a lot of assumptions on her behalf, neither of which are ever good ideas, but her actions revealed to my 20-year-old-arrogant-self that she viewed *her* paycheck as *her* money. *Her lack of giving must mean she has a lack of faith.* This story speaks more to my lack of maturity than her lack of faith.

Looking back on it, I'm pretty sure she was a new believer. She was just learning about giving. Doing the best she could.

After Nehemiah reintroduced the people of Jerusalem to God's Word, he moved to their tithes and offerings. This wasn't a matter of practicality, *We need supplies to make sure the house of the LORD has what it needs.* That was never the issue. God had already proven to Nehemiah at the very beginning of this book that He could provide for all the resources that would ever be needed. This was a matter of the heart. Nehemiah wanted the people under his care to view everything through the filter of God. This included their possessions and income.

Tithing

Tithe is a word that means "tenth part." It was established in the Old Testament as a practice of giving God *a tenth part* of everything through offerings. Today, tithing is an excellent way of acknowledging and reminding ourselves that what we have isn't really ours. We have jobs because God has allowed it. He has given us the ability to work. He is the One that sustains us, not our jobs. At any moment, He could bring a promotion into our lives or take our jobs away. He is in control, not us.

Ever use the word "my" in front of something? *My* car. *My* house. *My* wife. *My* kids. In a sense, those statements are undoubtedly true. You are the one responsible. On the other hand, God is the One that gave them to you. They are ultimately under His control. You are the steward, not the owner. Having this perspective will significantly help our perspective on "my" possessions.

Tithing is a way of our telling God *Thank You for what you have given me, and I realize I have what I do because of*

You. If you read through Nehemiah 10:34-38, you'll notice that what is asked to be given to God is "firsts." First fruits. First heads of cattle and herds. First of ground meal. The idea that Nehemiah is reinforcing is that we don't merely give God our leftovers. He gets our best. The first of what we have goes back to Him as an acknowledgment of His giving to us.

It has always been that way since the very first offering we saw in Genesis. Cain brought "some of the fruit" while Abel brought "the firstborn of his flock." God demonstrated His desires by His reaction. "The LORD looked with favor on Abel and His offering, but on Cain and his offering he did not look with favor," (Genesis 4:3-5).

God doesn't *need* our tithes. It's not like His bride, the church, would cease to exist if we quit putting money into the offering plates. When His disciples needed some money, Jesus pulled some coins out of a fish's mouth to pay their tax (Matthew 17:27). He doesn't ask us to tithe for His benefit. Tithing is for us. It has more to do with training our hearts than funding His work.

A cheerful giver

While the Old Testament teaches the practice of giving a tenth part as an offering, the idea is expanded upon in the New Testament. When it comes to tithing, we should give 10% of our income to our local church as an offering to God. A recognition that what I have is from Him. But I should also be open to other opportunities to give when the needs arise or as God leads.

A family we know is going through a tough time and needs a little help. Food banks running low on inventory. A horrific storm passes through our town and devastates much of the community. All of these are opportunities for giving. And that's what matters the most. *The giving.* Additionally, it's not just the fact that we give, but the heart behind it. The reasons and motivations. These seem to matter more than the amounts (2 Corinthians 9:7).

On one occasion, Jesus sat down in the temple across from the place where the offerings were put and watched as people walked past them (a bit of an intimidating situation, I'm sure). He saw people drop their offering into the treasury. And He looked on as many rich people tossed in large amounts. He never said a word about it. Then, a poor widow came through and dropped in a couple of coins that added up to practically nothing.

After she did so, Jesus called His disciples together, *Did you see that? That faithful lady right over there; she has given more as an offering than all the others.* Mathematically speaking, this woman barely gave a fraction of the amount other people had given. So, clearly, Jesus is not impressed with the amount of money we offer. What made Him point out her offering to His disciples was the heart behind her giving. Her offering cost her something. It mattered to her. It was a gift to God that would have been a sacrifice on her part (Mark 12:41-44).

Offerings as an act of worship

The whole of our Christian faith is centered around a sacrifice—Jesus willingly gave up His life to save the rest of us. It only makes sense that if we are to follow after the Son, we will have to live a life of sacrifice. This includes the area of our finances.

We can see this truth in the life of David. King David was building an altar to the LORD on a piece of property that belonged to another man, Araunah. When Araunah saw what was going on, David offered to buy the land. Araunah told David, probably because he was the king, that David could simply have the land. *No need to buy it.* David would have none of it. He insisted on buying the property because there was no way he would, "sacrifice to the LORD my God burnt offerings that cost me nothing" (2 Samuel 24:24).

We shouldn't simply give God a little bit of the surplus He has provided for us. Like David and the widow in the temple, our gift should cost us something. It should matter. And like all meaningful gifts we give to anyone, our offerings should be something we really think about and consider before giving.

Our offering is an act of worship. It reflects our heart. It also helps transform us to be more Christlike. If you spend any time at all reading through any parts of the Bible, the generosity of God is evident. All the good gifts we have come from Him (James 1:17). He gives freely and generously. When we give, whether to the church, other ministries and charities, or just people in need, we are taking on one of the characteristics of God. We are becoming more like Him, and that is the goal of our faith. To know and become more like Jesus.

The girl I briefly dated in college that gave a dollar, did actually give something. She was trying. She was learning to be obedient in her giving. As a new believer, giving anything at all might have felt like a sacrifice to her. And if it did, there's a great chance that Jesus looked more favorably on her gift that day than He did mine.

CONSIDER THESE QUESTIONS

- Does tithing come easily to you? Does it need work? What does your giving say about your heart?
- Other than your church, what are some other opportunities you think God may be leading you to support?
- How could "your" car/house/pantry/tools be opportunities for you to give to God?

25

BY KENT

The Godly Dad **PRAISES** God through Worship

"The musicians were under the king's orders, which regulated their daily activity."

NEHEMIAH 11:23

ONE OF MY ALL-TIME favorite bands is ELO. If you didn't know that stands for Electric Light Orchestra, then you and I are gonna have a *showdown*. You don't know a *livin' thing*, can't *hold on tight* to your dreams, and one day, you'll probably meet an *evil woman* and *turn to stone*. Better catch the *last train to London* and go ask *Mr. Blue Sky* for some help.

Here we are, three and four decades after some of their top songs hit the radio airwaves, and I'll still occasionally pull them up on Spotify and indoctrinate my children in the ways of the best rock and roll band ever. I know, fighting words.

I grew up on classic rock and eighties hair band music. Bands like the Eagles, REO Speedwagon, The Cars and Hall & Oates were always blaring from my Walkman and car stereo.

However, if I'm honest, a huge portion of that music, from a content standpoint, is not God honoring. Tons of the songs from that era glorify drunkenness, sexual promiscuity and drug use. Well, that was true of the songs that actually had a point. Many of those 80's songs, what in the world were they even talking about?

Those songs were a reflection of the beliefs and behaviors of the artists. Out of the overflow of the heart the mouth speaks. The same is true today. If we go browsing modern-day billboard charts, we'll find those themes dominate the biggest hits of our day as well. They've just gotten more visual and explicit. I suspect forty years from now, the themes will still be the same, and the visual exploits will be delivered via virtual reality. They'll be even more immersive and attractive to young minds.

I want to walk a fine line here. I'm not encouraging you to build a bonfire and throw all your old wax albums on it. They'd just melt anyway. But I do want to encourage you to be a critical consumer of what's allowed into your ears. And, particularly, what you allow to go into the ears of your family.

My tastes have changed

If you graph my life, you'll find two major time periods – Before Christ, and After Christ. Roughly speaking, my first twenty years were the B.C. period, and the last thirty have been the A.C. era. I came to know the LORD in college, and the most influential person in my life during that season was my girlfriend April (who's now been my lovely bride for twenty-five years!). One thing was evident about us early on – we had very different musical influences.

Sure, she'd enjoy a good Beatles or Queen song now and then, but she spent most of her time listening to Stephen Curtis Chapman, DC Talk, Michael W. Smith and Amy Grant. When I first became a believer in Christ, I didn't even know things like "Christian music" existed. I was surprised to hear of this genre, and at first, it was a tug of war.

I would listen to some Christian music, then chase it down with a smash hit from Def Leppard or Aerosmith. I enjoyed all of it, and to a degree, still do.

However, if you could look on my life chart, you'd see a tradeoff happening. Over the last thirty years, I've listened to far less "secular" music and far more "Christian" music. And, on this topic, again allow me to remind you – I'm not trying to convince you that listening to non-christian music is evil or will send you to hell. I am trying to remind you of this: what you allow into your mind actually matters.

Psalm 101:3 says, "I will not set before my eyes anything that is worthless. I hate the work of those who fall away, it shall not cling to me." I believe this same principle applies to our ears as well. God's word has declared it for thousands of years, and modern brain research is validating it over and over again. What we watch and listen to affects our brains, for better or worse.

Serious about worship

Nehemiah was serious about worship. Now, worship in a general sense means more than music or singing. True worship is an act of the heart and it comes in many forms. But, look closely at Nehemiah 11. It says, *"The musicians were under the king's orders, which regulated their daily activity."* In the ESV, it's described as a fixed provision for the singers they received every day.

He made sure that those who could sing and play music were amply supplied. Not only that, when the wall was being dedicated, Nehemiah put on a massive worship concert to celebrate.

Nehemiah 12:27-43 describes this ceremony with some powerful visual details. Nehemiah assembled many of the leaders and then instructed them to go up on top of the wall ("Hope we built this thing correctly!"). He appointed two "great choirs" and sent them off in opposite directions to file along the top of the wall (Nehemiah 12: 31). Some of them had trumpets (12:35) and other instruments (12:36). He and Ezra accompanied them.

Picture this event in your mind. Imagine you're standing in the center of Jerusalem. Around you, there's a giant boundary wall, several thousand feet in length, a story or two high, with people standing atop it. They have come to sing and worship God. They rejoiced, sang, and shouted their praises so loudly that, "the joy of Jerusalem was heard far away." (Nehemiah 12:43 ESV).

To celebrate their new city wall, they worshipped. Loudly. All together. Led by their musicians and singers. Nehemiah knew this would honor God and mark their memories with the indelible ink of an unforgettable event.

Stacking the deck

To Nehemiah, music mattered, and he leveraged it to honor God. I bet most of us would agree, worshiping by singing *in church* or at a Christian concert is a great idea. But, some recent research may help you see this from a wider angle.

If you're a dad like me, you want to hand down your faith to your children. Or, at least, give them every opportunity to accept it. You would like to make the path to God and Jesus obvious and remove any roadblocks that your children may hit along their way. Would it surprise you to learn that one of those roadblocks can be the kind of music you're playing around your house?

The team at LifeWay Research did a study that helped us understand what factors influence our kids' faith decisions after they leave our house. They looked at factors which made the children more likely to keep walking in the Christian faith, and those that pushed them away.

One of the top four positive influences was that the "Child regularly listened to Christian music while growing up." Reading the Bible regularly was a decisive top factor. But, closely behind was nearly a three-way tie between praying, serving in church and listening to Christian music. Conversely, the third most common negative predictor was when a child regularly listened to secular music.[2]

For parents, the implications are obvious. Drench them in God's word. Teach them to pray. Encourage them to serve at church. Expose them to wholesome Christian music. These are the top four parenting moves we can make to position our kids to find their way. This is much easier to do when we're doing those things ourselves.

More of our values are caught than taught. If we're living a life that exhibits these same behaviors, our children are more likely to pick up those same behaviors. Just look at sports affiliations in families. If you're an Auburn fan, odds are, your kids will be too. And, heaven forbid they cheer for Alabama. Over your dead body.

Why do these affiliations usually trend down our family tree? Because during any given year in our child's life, they might hear hundreds of positive references to "our team," and dozens of negative comments about "those losers" on the other side. They pick up on our values, preferences and arguments for our point of view.

---

2   https://lifewayresearch.com/2017/10/17/young-bible-readers-more-likely-to-be-faithful-adults-study-finds

When we routinely play worship or Christian music in our homes and cars, we're sending signals. Well, sound waves. We're scattering audible seeds into the minds of our children. Over time, they tend to take root and produce fruit.

When my oldest son was just a couple years old, my wife and I sensed there was a battle afoot for his mind and heart. Not just because he went through the "terrible two's." In fact, his were more like the terrible fours through nines. Anyhow, the point is, we just had a gnawing feeling that as a young boy, he was under attack.

One way we decided to combat this was with music. We had a small CD player and radio combo in his bedroom, and during his naps, playtime and when putting him down for bed, we had it playing all the time. About ten percent of the time, we played classical music. The other ninety percent, it was worship music or modern Christian music.

He grew up listening to a little bit of Bach, and a ton of Newsboys, Avalon, Chris Rice, Rich Mullins and For King & Country.

Now, he's married to a lovely young lady and they're just staring their life out together. Guess what? She's an amazing cello player and music major. And, our son's a fellow music major with his eye on either a studio musician or worship leader career. Go figure.

Nehemiah was serious about music and worship.

Let's join in one chorus and agree with him.

CONSIDER THESE QUESTIONS

- When you consider those top four LifeWay Research factors, which ones do you implement regularly? Which ones could use some newfound emphasis?

- What are the musical influences that have shaped your life? What did you grow up listening to? Can you imagine ways it positively or negatively affected you?

- How often do you and your family worship together? Ever? Do you go different directions at church? If so, what might happen if you created some "worship moments" from time to time that you and your family share together?

26

BY ERIC

The Godly Dad **PURIFIES** His Home from Evil

> "I gave orders to purify the rooms, and then I put back into them the equipment of the house of God..."
>
> *NEHEMIAH 13:9*

IN COLLEGE, BECAUSE THERE were no mountains where we lived, my friends and I searched for different structures we could climb. Restaurants, office buildings, fire towers, bridges, train trusses. Anything we could scale.

One night we found a long bridge that stretched over a nearby river about 50-60 feet above the water. We would often take a detour off-road towards the underside of the bridge.

Then we would back my jeep up to the base of the bridge so that we could reach the iron ladder mounted to the huge pillar. From there, we would walk across the catwalk to the next base pillar that held the bridge up at the bank of the river and rappel down. We would repeat this process for hours.

One night, we took my friend's girlfriend and her roommate with us. After a night of climbing and rappelling, as we were leaving, my jeep got stuck in some mud. My friend and the two girls got out to push while I tried to steer us clear of the mud. Just as I broke free of the mud, I heard one of the girls, Kristina, scream as if she was dying. I had never murdered anyone with my jeep before, but I didn't feel the kind of bump you'd expect as the tires roll over the body. Frantically, I hopped out of the jeep and ran to the back to check on Kristina. Apparently, she was standing directly behind one of the back wheels as she was pushing the vehicle. She got sprayed with mud. She looked up at me and asked, "How bad is it? How muddy am I?" It was dark, which made it difficult to see and know for sure, but she didn't look too bad. "I think you're alright," I told her. "It probably just felt worse than it actually is." We all climbed back into the jeep and drove home.

As I parked in front of our apartment, the porch light was on and shone through my windshield. It gave Kristina a better look at the filth that covered her. She screamed again. Pushing her way out of the jeep, she ran under the porch light to get a better look. Under the bridge and in the dark, it looked like Kristina only had a little bit of mud on her legs, but standing in the light, it became quite clear she was covered in mud. It was everywhere. She kept screaming, "Uggg, I'm so gross! I have to wash this mess off now!" Only when we come into the light do we notice how much filth has accumulated on us.

After his first term as governor, Nehemiah left Jerusalem for some time. When he returned, he found that the people had turned back to their old ways. Without hesitation, Nehemiah got back to work, setting things right. He started in the temple.

Eliashib, the high priest, had given Tobiah, an enemy of Nehemiah and his restoration work of Jerusalem, a room in one of the temple chambers so he could store his stuff there. Tobiah turned the temple of God into his personal warehouse. This meant he could continue influencing people away from God and could now do it from directly within the temple of God. Nehemiah would have none of it. He began purifying the temple by tossing Tobiah's junk out on the street. But he didn't stop there. Nehemiah ordered for all the rooms to be cleaned from the spiritual stains left from the presence of the unbeliever. Then, once everything had been purified, Nehemiah restored the temple to the state it was intended.

Cleaning house

As godly fathers, sometimes we have to *clean house*. We have to take an honest look at our family and around our homes to see what kind of spiritual junk we've allowed to creep its way in. But when we do this, the first honest look we should take is one right into a mirror.

What kind of evil clutter have we allowed to gather in our own hearts? What bad habits, that we once considered disgraceful, have become a common practice of ours? We need God's perspective to gauge our personal evaluation effectively. Like Kristina under the bridge, when we are living in areas of darkness, it's easy to think *Well, there may be a little bit of dirt here and there, but it's really not that bad.* But the moment we step into the light of God's truth, it becomes quite clear just how sinful we are. We're covered with dirt and desperately need to be made clean.

Repentance will be our first step. It is more profound than a feeling of regret or sorrow. In the Biblical sense of the word, "to repent" means to turn around and head in a different direction. The definition suggests the idea of walking down the wrong path, realizing the mistake you are making, and then correcting it by turning around and walking in the opposite direction. That's a good visual representation of repentance.

Before we start removing the spiritual garbage in our lives and those of our family members, we must realize the wrong path it is leading us down. Tossing the junk out is part of the repentance process. Nehemiah had a zero-tolerance policy for wicked rubbish, and so should we.

The effects of sinful garbage

When the literal trash in your house starts to pile up, you can smell it. Even when you can't see it, you know it's there. The putrid odor permeates the room even if you can't pinpoint where the garbage is. And the only way to get rid of the lingering smell is to remove the source of it. The same is true when spiritual garbage starts to build up. Our family may not see us do the things we shouldn't do, but they can sense the effects. They notice the changes that our undealt-with-sins have wrought on us. Whether we become distant, short-tempered, absent, indifferent, depressed, or angry all the time, those close to us will notice. They'll smell the garbage on us even if they can't see the source of it.

This purifying process of *cleaning house* will be both spiritual and physical. During one of Jacob's encounters with God, the LORD told Jacob to return to Bethel, build an altar to God, and settle in that land. The first thing Jacob did before the journey back home began was to tell his whole household, "Get rid of the foreign gods you have with you, and purify yourselves…" He then took their false idols and buried them in the ground so no one could find them (Genesis 35:2-4). Jacob was cleaning house. He took the physical objects that led to spiritual separation from God and trashed them.

What physical items around the house are leading us away from God? Television channels showing things we shouldn't see? Magazines stashed around, filling our minds with junk? Items tucked in the cabinets, slowly pulling us towards addiction? Whatever it is, it's got to go! To be repentant, we have to toss that junk out and walk away from it.

If I could drive by your house this week, what should I notice piled in your front yard for the garbage pickup folks to take away?

The repentant example

As godly fathers, we are setting an example for our kids of what a godly man is supposed to look like. And we are the *primary* example they will see day in and day out for years. Our model teaches our sons what kind of men they are supposed to grow to become. We are their mental picture of a Christian man. We show them how a godly man talks, carries himself and treats others. And, when it's needed, we teach them how a godly man repents from mistakes.

Equally as important, our example teaches our daughters what kind of men they should allow in their lives. They learn how they are to be treated by how we treat them and their mother. If spiritual garbage leads us to be disrespectful to our wives, our daughters will think it's okay for guys to disrespect them.

Nehemiah wasted no time purifying the temple because the negative effect it was having on the people was devastating. It was undoing everything he had worked so hard to establish before he left. Unchecked sin can have disastrous effects.

The truth is, we can put in place the same kind of impediments to our children's spiritual growth. If they discover some undealt-with spiritual garbage we've allowed to stack up, it has the potential to undo everything we have tried to teach them about following after God. They will see us differently. Hear our words differently. Or not at all. We must fight with all we have never to reach that point. Whenever we start to see the spiritual dirt beginning to collect, we must take action. We must *clean house*. Like Nehemiah, we have to do whatever it takes to cleanse the temple of our homes.

CONSIDER THESE QUESTIONS

- What evil clutter have we allowed to gather in our hearts and homes? What effect is it having on us? On our family?

- Do your kids have any wicked garbage around that is stinking up their lives? What do you need to do to help them dispose of it?

- How can you demonstrate repentance to your family? What do you think the benefit of doing this could be?

27

BY ERIC

The Godly Dad REBUKES Those Who Wander

"So I rebuked the officials and asked them, 'Why is the house of God neglected?'... "

NEHEMIAH 13:11

HAVE YOU EVER STARTED out in one direction, but then felt like God was telling you to change course?

When I started college, it was as an engineering student. During the summer between my sophomore and junior year, I felt God call me into the ministry, so I switched majors. My new major required me to take a statistics class. After all the calculus classes I had already taken, statistics was a breeze. I didn't make anything lower than a 96 on the exams.

Halfway through the semester, the professor called me to her desk before class started. "Eric, I know you know this material. It's evident by your test scores. But if you don't do your homework, I'm going to give you a C for this class regardless of your test scores." *Okay* is all I said. "I don't think you understand," she continued, "if you want an A, you're going to have to do your homework." "Oh, I get it," I said with a little too much indifference in my voice. With a puzzled look on her face, she looked me straight in the eyes and pushed, "Are you going to do your homework?" "I don't know," I answered, which was a lie. I already knew I wasn't going to do my homework. True to her word, I made a C in statistics after making high A's on all the tests.

My statistics professor was trying to gently rebuke my lazy behavior with her assignments. She saw my potential for success and wanted to get me on the right path. Unfortunately, I wasn't a big fan of school at the time and didn't follow her corrections. It cost me in the end.

When Nehemiah saw people straying from their commitments to God, he went to the officials and held them accountable. They had been left in charge. Nehemiah rebuked them for their lack of regard for their responsibilities. They were the ones who were supposed to be leading the people in the right direction. Instead, they wandered away from their path as well. Nehemiah gave them a quick correction.

Responsibilities were being half-heartedly attempted or wholly ignored. The priests were being neglected. Those in charge of leading the religious ceremonies quit, returning to their old lives (13:10). Nehemiah, to get things back on track, replaced some of the priests and scribes with men he considered trustworthy. These measures of discipline would have been hurtful and embarrassing to those being rebuked. But it had to be done.

The need for correction

Correction is a necessary part of being a parent. Our parents are the first ones that ever teach us the difference between right and wrong. They are the ones that help us understand what is acceptable and what isn't. They set the boundaries. Of course, as kids, we push these boundaries to see precisely where the limits are. This is something we always knew, but our grasp on the concept has become much more significant now that we are parents ourselves. Nothing can teach you more about your father than becoming a father yourself.

As godly fathers, we are now tasked with setting those boundaries. We help guide our kids to learn the differences between right and wrong. What brings honor to God and what doesn't. And when our kids begin to wander too far from that path, it's our responsibility to bring them back. To correct their actions and choices. It has to be done for their benefit. My statistics professor tried to gently warn me that my choices were leading me away from an A I could have had. She did it for my benefit, not hers. She was trying to help. Correction should be an act of love.

Loving correction

We rebuke our kids because we love them. We want the best for them. When they start to drift away into dangerous choices, we step in to correct their course. But this must be done gently and in love. Love should be the driving force behind every one of our rebukes. The reason God corrects and disciplines us is because He loves us. "My son, do not despise the LORD's discipline, and do not resent his rebuke, because the LORD disciplines those he loves, as a father the son he delights in" (Proverbs 3:11-12).

I stress this point of correction coming from a place of love because when our rebuking words are spoken out loud to our kids, they rarely sound like love. When we feel like we have been pushed and pushed past our limits, our emotions start running high. When we finally approach our kids, our correction comes out more like an explosion than a gentle rebuke. This tends to have the opposite effect on our kids than we desire. Resentment, instead of respect, is birthed.

Because rebukes, even delivered in love, can be painful, we must present them gently (Galatians 6:1). If you have toddlers in the house, you may have to slap their little hands when they reach for a hot stove. That small sting of a slapped hand prevents a much more significant pain and possible permanent damage from a burnt hand. The rebuke is painful but necessary. And it is done gently. You don't slap their hand as hard as you can. The same is true for their more mature mistakes. Our rebukes and correction may be painful to them at first, but it is given to prevent more devastating and possibly permanent damage. Maybe even eternal (James 5:20). Because we know this, we rebuke gently instead of hurting them as much as we can. It's an act of love.

There's a right and wrong time

While correction is a needed part of fatherhood, we don't need to correct *everything*. Our primary focus should be rebuking our kids when they wander away from God's commands, not all our personal preferences. Hopefully, our *house laws* line up with God's Law, but that doesn't make them one and the same. We shouldn't try to twist God's Word into backing up our personal rules.

I've known guys who are adamantly against tattoos and piercings of any kind. Because of their strong opinion of this "wickedness," they'll quote 1 Corinthians 6:19-20 to their kids, "Do you not know that your bodies are temples of the Holy Spirit, who is in you, whom you have received from God? You are not your own; you were bought at a price. Therefore honor God with your bodies." *Scaring up your body is damaging God's temple and not honoring Him with your body.* Getting piercings and tattoos does technically harm the body, but so does candy. And a second helping around the dinner table. So, let's be real careful about what we present to our kids as God's commands.

I'm not saying don't have your own personal rules for your house. How you raise your kids will be different than how I raise mine. And that's okay. You may have no problem allowing your kids to support the evils of the Ole Miss Rebels. It's simply unacceptable in my house. What I'm saying is that if our commands – the absolute issues we won't compromise on – are tied to God's commandments, we have an unshakable foundation to point to and build upon. God is seen as the ultimate authority. But when our commands are tied only to our opinions of right and wrong, we make ourselves the final authority.

Nitpicking every one of our kids' choices to line up with our personal preferences will only push them away from us. It will exasperate them (Ephesians 6:4). It's best to set God up as the ultimate authority in the lives of our children. Not us. Plus, He's a much better Father than we could ever be.

We mustn't stop at rebuking our children. We must also help them find their way back from where they strayed. After Nehemiah rebuked the temple officials, he then, "called them together and stationed them at their posts," (Nehemiah 13:11). He rebuked them, then got them positioned back to the places they were meant to be.

If all we do is point out our children's mistakes and shortcomings with no guidance or help on how to get back to where they are meant to be, we're not much of a disciple-maker. Jesus corrected His disciples, *then* showed them a better way. There's got to be both correction and guidance for significant growth to take root.

- How do you typically correct your kids? Afterward, do you think they walk away feeling loved or torn apart? How can you ensure they see the love behind all your corrections?

- What are the absolute "non-negotiable" rules of your house? Are all those tied to God's Word? Should they be? Why or why not?

- After you rebuke your kids, how do you help guide them back to the path they should walk down?

28

BY ERIC

The Godly Dad **SACRIFICES** for God's Purpose

"...do not blot out what I have so faithfully done for the house of my God and its services."

NEHEMIAH 13:14

IN THE TENTH GRADE, our group of friends all bought paintball guns. We spent plenty of weekends that year playing a paint-ball version of capture the flag in some wooded acres next to our friend's house. I like to think that I'm good at paintball, capture the flag, and any other war-like games, but truth be told, I am usually one of the first ones out.

During one of our epic games, I was flanking the enemy when someone screamed from behind me, "He's got our flag! Get him!" At the time, I didn't know who "him" was, and I wasn't exactly sure who had even screamed out the instructions, but I saw a figure running through the woods on my left, so I chased after him.

Weaving through trees and over logs, I raced behind this guy like a mad man. Every stride pushed me closer. Determination helped me close the gap until I was finally close enough to tackle him. We rolled over each other, and I rose to my feet in victory. "I got him!" I yelled back to our base. "No, you didn't!" a voice echoed back. "We lost." The guy I tackled looked up at me with a smile on his face and showed me his empty hands. He didn't have the flag. He was the decoy. I had been chasing the wrong guy the whole time, and it cost my team and me the game.

Nehemiah had a pretty sweet job before his rebuild-the-wall project started in Jerusalem. Cupbearer to the king had its fair share of perks. He was an official of King Artaxerxes, which had to have been beneficial. It was a comfortable job. Steady. Dangerous, but hardly laborious. Nehemiah may have even lived in the palace.

But he gave all that up so he could restore the broken-down city and people of Jerusalem. The work was hard. The people were difficult. Nehemiah made enemies, which made the new task even more dangerous. Anytime you have to do your work with one hand while you hold a weapon for protection in the other, your job is precarious, to say the least. Why would Nehemiah do this? Why give up the comfortable in exchange for the burdensome?

The choice of sacrifice

Nehemiah walked away from a life that would better serve him and his needs so that he could embrace a life of serving his God. It was a choice of sacrifice. And Nehemiah's sacrifices for God's purpose made all the difference for the people living in Jerusalem and the walls that protected them.

Whether you realize it or not, you live your life making sacrifices on almost a daily basis. There's no question about that. We give up a little of our health so we can have those burgers and fries. We give up time with our family to stay a little later at the office. We give up buying something for ourselves so our kids can get braces. Almost every choice can be seen as a sacrifice. You give up one thing to gain another. The only real question is, are the things you gain worth more than the things you give up? Is what you chase after worth the sacrifices of the pursuit? If you're not careful, you can end up like me in our Capture the Flag game and spend your whole life chasing after the wrong thing. Nehemiah gave up a cushy life to pursue a godly purpose. And while serving under the king certainly had its benefits, only serving the King of kings produces eternal benefits. A prize of infinite value.

Men of sacrifice

If you read through the Bible, you'll see that all the great men that fill its pages were men of sacrifice. Almost as if it were a prerequisite. Maybe it is.

Abraham gave up all he knew and the comforts of home so that he could follow God into the unknown (Genesis 12:1, 4). Even though he had no idea where he was going or what he'd be doing, he knew he was answering God's calling. So, Abraham packed his bags and left. Years later, God would ask Abraham for another sacrifice. This one would come by way of him giving up his son Isaac (Geneses 22:2). This test of faith was to prove to Abraham that God was the most important thing in his life. There was nothing Abraham wouldn't surrender to God, not even his son. His constant sacrifices to the LORD's calling led Abraham to become the father of God's chosen people.

While walking the banks of the Sea of Galilee, Jesus called out to Peter and Andrew, who were at their "office" at the time, working their nets. "Come, follow me," Jesus said, "and I will send you out to fish for people" (Mark 1:17). The fishermen's response was to drop their nets *at once* and follow Jesus. Peter and Andrew left more than their jobs. This was their business. One they owned. Chances are, it was passed down from generation to generation to them. They probably grew up learning to fish that lake from their father and maybe even grandfather. They would have been good at it. Comfortable. And they left all that behind when Jesus called them to follow

Him. Left it all on the beach to become the men Jesus would transform them into.

The apostle Paul, when he was still known as Saul, was a young rockstar Pharisee quickly rising through the ranks of the religious leaders (Philippians 3:4-6). His position came with a lot of respect in his community. The title of *teacher*. The place of honor at banquets. The most important seat in the synagogues (Matthew 23:6-7). Saul was *somebody*. He gave all that up to chase after the life Christ had called him towards. And he never looked back.

He considered that old life, one filled with worldly success, to be a wasted one. Garbage. "But whatever were gains to me I now consider loss for the sake of Christ. What is more, I consider everything a loss because of the surpassing worth of knowing Christ Jesus my Lord, for whose sake I have lost all things. I consider them garbage, that I may gain Christ," (Philippians 3:7-8).

A treasured sacrifice

So, what is it? What is God calling you to give up or leave behind so that you can follow Him more closely? Whatever it is, say *yes*. Put away the desire for earthly rewards so you can pursue the things of eternal worth. The stuff here on this side of eternity never lasts and isn't worth our life's ambition. Whatever we chase after consumes us. It will have our hearts (Matthew 6:19-21). Make sure your treasure hunt is worth the cost of who you are.

Put down the T.V. remote and pick up the LEGO set with your son. Leave work early enough so you can make it to your daughter's basketball game on time. Make your life truly matter. No one lays in their hospital bed with only moments left of their lives and declares to those gathered around them, *I wish I had more money right now.* Nor do they ever say *If only I had a few more hours to check and send some work emails.* That stuff doesn't matter at the end of our lives because it never truly mattered in the first place.

What we treasure reveals what we have stored up in our hearts. Because of this, our lives are an investment. Our actions become transactions. Let's place some down payments on eternity. When God's voice rings out, searching for someone to carry out His will and purposes for our family, let our voices echo that of Isaiah's, "Here am I. Send me!" (Isaiah 6:8).

If you and I want to become godly dads, we will have to make sacrifices for God's purpose. We will have to surrender our desires to take on the desires of God. We will give up what makes us comfortable to follow Jesus into the unknown. But that is exactly where He will be found. In the mystery. It is in the unknown and the uncomfortable that our faith takes over. We let go of ourselves and take hold of God. It will be a sacrifice. But one that is overwhelmingly worth it.

I doubt Nehemiah ever longed for the life he gave up. The things he left behind. I'm sure he was too focused on the glorious opportunities he had to lead his people closer to God. This should be our approach as well. What we give up will never compare to the riches of leading our families to the feet of Jesus. Discipling our family as fathers is the greatest calling God has placed in our lives. A sacrifice we want to make. And like it did for Nehemiah and the people of Jerusalem, our sacrifices will make all the difference in our lives. And the lives of those around us.

CONSIDER THESE QUESTIONS

- How is being a godly dad a commitment to a life of sacrifice?
- What sacrifices have you had to make as a father? What godly sacrifices do you still need to make?
- How do you want your family to remember you? What do you need to start doing now to ensure that legacy is the one they remember?

EPILOGUE

Building our Family Wall

THE LAST LINE NEHEMIAH penned in his book was, "Remember me with favor, my God," (13:31). His final thought. Probably, his final request. He wanted his legacy to be intertwined with God's calling on his life.

So, how do you want to be remembered? Do you want people to huddle around at your funeral and say, *Man, am I going to miss that guy! He had the best handicap in golf*! Or maybe there's a guy there who will be relieved he finally has a chance to win your fantasy sports league because *the guy that spent all his time on his hobby is now gone*. Now that you've read this book, maybe you're hoping those you leave behind will decide to write on your tombstone, *"World's greatest dad and husband."* That's how you *want* to be remembered. That kind of legacy isn't reached accidentally. It takes effort. Sacrifice. A heart searching for God's strength by crying out, *Remember me with favor, my God.*

Nehemiah was a man. By every definition of the word, Nehemiah embodied manhood. Strong. Wise. Loving. Disciplined. He consistently gave of himself to protect those under his care. He fought to keep the enemy outside the walls that guarded his people. He led by example. He made the tough decisions. He wasn't interrupted by distraction. He was the one everyone else could look to for guidance and direction. Dependable. Like the apostle Paul, Nehemiah could have confidently said: *Follow my example as I follow after God* (1 Corinthians 11:1). All those traits make for a good father. A godly father.

The lessons in this book we learned from Nehemiah have armed us with the tools we need to be the kind of fathers God has called us to be. But understanding Nehemiah's example isn't enough. We have to follow it. Put it into practice. Nehemiah was remembered favorably for what he *did* for others in leading them toward God. You'll be remembered favorably because of all your Godward investments in your family. *Wanting* to be a good dad is a solid sentiment. Allowing that desire to drive *the actions* of a good father is what creates memories. Legacies.

Give Nehemiah's principles a try. Some of his traits you probably already possess. But some you may have never even heard of. Pick one or two of those areas and get to work. And it will be work. Hard work. But, as Theodore Roosevelt said, "Nothing in the world is worth having or worth doing unless it means effort, pain, difficulty…I have never in my life envied a human being who led an easy life. I have envied a great many people who led difficult lives and led them well."

Being a godly father will not lead to an easy life.

But it will be a life worth remembering.

You're not a father on accident.
So, go be a Father On Purpose.

What would it mean to your family if you were a father who lived fully *on purpose*? Imagine waking up every day with a gleam in your eye and a spring in your step, ready to lead confidently and intentionally. This can be you.

However, this world is working against you. Endless distractions, temptations and lies from our enemy combine to make us completely exhausted. We tap out and forfeit as a dad. We raise the white flag and surrender. It's easier just to keep our heads down and put in our hours on the job than to fight the good fight at home every day.

Father On Purpose can help you get back in the game. This is a community of dads who want to raise godly children in a rough and tumble world. To do this, we band together. We learn from one another so we can discover what works well, and what doesn't.

Being a dad is too important to go it alone.

Come join us.

www.fatheronpurpose.org

We Help Dads Disciple Their Sons.

Are you a father of sons between the ages of 8 and 18? If you are, you're in a battle. A spiritual battle for the hearts and minds of your boys is raging. Know why? Because they're the fathers of tomorrow.

One of the greatest legacies you can leave this world are godly fathers coming right behind you. In many ways, it's the greatest earthly hope this world has. Men who can love and lead their families well.

Manhood Journey exists to help you intentionally disciple your boys. We provide resources – Bible studies, eBooks, reading plans and digital courses – to help you faithfully lead and prepare your young men for an adulthood that will honor God. You may not feel like you have the tools, training or qualifications to be a future-godly-father-maker.

We can help you get there.

Learn more: **www.manhoodjourney.org**

Where are you on your godly fatherhood journey?

Are you a dad who wants to be a godly father, but you're just not sure where you are right now on that journey; and, you don't know what next step to take to make progress?

We've built a tool just for you. It's the Godly Father Assessment.

This free and confidential online resource helps you figure out how you're doing in two ways:

- 7 Behaviors – there are seven behaviors – or skill sets – that godly dads strive to master. The Godly Father Assessment will show you what those seven things are and explain them clearly.

- 4 Stages – we're all works in progress and at different stages in our journey. This assessment will help you figure out where you are right now so you can chart your next steps to make meaningful progress.

In addition to getting customized and personalized results, you'll get specific recommendations for next-step resources that can help you become an even godlier father than you are right now.

Take the assessment today! It's FREE!

www.manhoodjourney.org/godly-father-assessment

234 | KENT EVANS & ERIC BALLARD

OTHER BOOKS BY KENT EVANS

Wise Guys: Unlocking Hidden Wisdom from the Men Around You

For guys, more than ever, it's a confusing world. Your GPS doesn't offer any maps showing how to get to the point of wisdom – and who likes asking for directions anyway? The answers may be all around you, in the form of guys you already know. Could there be ways to tap into their invaluable knowledge without enduring dull lectures or taking pages of notes? Kent Evans has surrounded himself with these wise guys. With a great deal of humor and an endless supply of stories, he wants to show you how to gather life-enriching truth from the guys in your own circle.

LEARN MORE
http://bit.ly/kentevanswiseguys

The Manhood Journey: Setting a Course for Godly Fatherhood

Biblical fatherhood cannot be outsourced. Fathers are the primary disciple makers in the home. Our children are following our lead, but where are we leading them? Are we leading them towards the perfect Father, encouraging them to grow in their faith and to become the adults that God made them to be? What does a godly dad look like? Kent Evans will help you become a confident, engaged father who leads his family with no regrets.

LEARN MORE
http://bit.ly/kentevansmjbook

OTHER BOOKS BY ERIC BALLARD

Art of Survival

Within every heart echoes a calling for something wild. Something adventurous. Something *more*. Even if you don't quite know what that *something* more is, you know it's out there. And elusive as it may be, you know it can be found. Two high school guys set out to explore the wild in search of a primitive calling while they hike the Appalachian Trail. Witness God's words come alive through their wild adventures wrestling with nature and what it means to follow God. A devotional for both girls and boys, *The Art of Survival* will be a daily Bible study that draws you in as you explore and encounter the Bible in ways you never have before.

LEARN MORE
http://bit.ly/ericballardsurvival

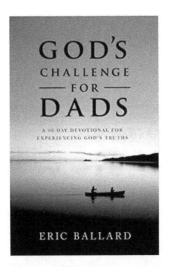

God's Challenge for Dads: A 90-Day Devotional Experiencing God's Truths

Have you gotten comfortable—maybe even complacent—in your spiritual life? Maybe you can check off all the right boxes—going to church, reading your Bible, praying before meals. Maybe you even lead a small group or serve as a deacon and tithe regularly. But when was the last time someone really shook up your faith, really challenged you to get after it, to pursue God with your *whole* heart? In this devotional written specifically for dads, Eric Ballard draws wisdom from the men written about in the Bible to push you out of your comfort zone and into a more authentic, whole-hearted relationship with God, which will lead to more meaningful relationships with your family, coworkers, and community.

LEARN MORE
http://bit.ly/ericballardchallenge

OTHER BOOKS FROM MANHOOD JOURNEY PRESS

More Than the Score

More than ever, youth sports has become a hypercompetitive battleground. Coaches berate the players and parents threaten the coaches. Pat Combs has seen first-hand the destruction this has caused. It's negatively impacting our homes and communities. This book gives you practical tools so you can breakdown the "win at all costs" paradigm and replace it with a growth mindset. Since almost all youth athletes will not become professional players, let's allow sports to give them something they can use their whole life: character and virtue. Traits that matter more than the score.

LEARN MORE
http://bit.ly/patcombsbook

ABOUT THE AUTHOR

PAT COMBS spent 8 years playing professional baseball for the Philadelphia Phillies (1st Round selection, 1988) and Milwaukee Brewers. As a collegiate athlete, Pat represented his country as a baseball player for Team USA. Pat was an All-American and Academic All-American at Baylor University.

Currently, Pat is a behavioral analytics consultant for numerous professional athletes, MLB & NFL teams, and corporate leaders. He is also a Director of a wealth management firm. He's a broadcast color analyst for Fox Sports college baseball and serves on multiple corporate and nonprofit boards. He and his wife, Christina, have 3 sons. Pat continues to mentor & coach young men in Southlake, Texas.

CPSIA information can be obtained
at www.ICGtesting.com
Printed in the USA
BVHW090852030322
630565BV00017B/387